Lands of our Ancestors: Three Generations
(Historical Novel in Three Parts)

Ethnic Studies
Teacher's Guide

Developed by
Elizabeth Sinclair and Gary Robinson

© 2016-2024
Tribal Eye Productions
P.O. Box 1123 / Santa Ynez, CA 93460
www.LandsOfOurAncestors.com

C 2016-2024 Tribal Eye Productions
ISBN 979-8-9887862-9-0
All Rights Reserved

TABLE OF CONTENTS

Teachers Guide Introduction

The teacher's guide is separated into the three historical eras: Spanish mission, Mexican rancho, and American colonial. Each section includes the same features: historical background, student worksheets, answer keys, and student project ideas.

The historical background supports both history and English teachers. Before diving into **Lands of Our Ancestors**, it is helpful to read this section to understand the major events and how they impacted people in California. This section pays particular attention to the Indian perspective which is often left out of history books. The section also includes images that help bring the history to life. Finally, for further reading, there is a list of additional resources.

Next are student-guided reading worksheets for each chapter of the book. The questions can be used in teacher-directed class discussions, small group discussions, or as written work. Each worksheet incorporates the six levels of questions: knowledge, comprehension, application, analysis, synthesis, and evaluation. The worksheets cover key terms, activities, and questions. The answer keys are in the back.

The last section of the teacher's guide includes class discussion questions and student project ideas. The open-ended discussion questions are related to the major Ethnic Studies themes and English and History standards. They are designed to be revisited throughout the book, and the projects are designed to meet the needs of diverse learners.

Ethnic Studies poses two big questions: How have race and ethnicity been constructed in America? And, how does ethnicity continue to shape America today? Answers to these questions are found by examining four major themes.

Ethnic Studies Standards

ES 1 - Identity
1. What factors shape identity? What parts of identities do we choose for ourselves and what parts are determined by others, society or chance?
2. What dilemmas arise when others view us differently than we view ourselves?
3. How do our identities influence our choices and the choices available to us?
4. What factors influence our identity and, in turn, the choices we make?

ES 2 - History & Movement
1. What does it mean to live on the land? Who may become an American? What happens when multiple narratives are layered on top of each other?
2. How should societies integrate newcomers? How do newcomers develop a sense of belonging to the places where they have arrived?
3. How does migration affect the identities of individuals, communities, and nations? What role have immigrants played in defining notions of democracy?
4. How do ideas or narratives about who may belong in a nation affect immigration policy, the lives of immigrants, and host communities?

ES 3 - Systems of Power
1. What is the relationship between individuals and society?
2. How does society divide people into groups? What are the implications for a society when it categorizes people into a social hierarchy?
3. What is the relationship between individual power and collective power?
4. How do social systems influence the choices we make?

ES 4 - Resistance Movements & Equity
1. How have social movements addressed different kinds of discrimination or oppression? What debates and dilemmas remain unresolved?
2. What debates and dilemmas from past historical movements remain unresolved? Why?
3. What is equity and why does it matter? What is the difference between equality and equity?
4. How can one make a difference in the community? What skills and tools are needed to create change in society?
5. It is appropriate to include a community engagement project that empowers students to use their knowledge and voice to effect social change.

What is Historical Fiction?

Lands of Our Ancestors is a work of historical fiction. While the characters are made up, the historical events and as much of their experiences as possible are based on historical facts. Authors use historical fiction to tell a story about what life might have felt like during this time. What happens to the Chumash characters in Lands of our Ancestors is typical of what may have happened to all the tribal people who came into contact with any missions built on their ancestral lands. Following these characters, their children, and grandchildren through this devastating century in California history brings the personal impact to life in a way that nonfiction cannot. Imagine their first impressions of the Spanish padres and soldiers and the debates they might have had about joining the missions. Imagine what it would be like to live at the missions, presidios, and settlements as forced labor.

Historical research is critical to telling a complete and accurate story. But what is 'the truth'? **Facts**, such as dates, places, names, about historical events are most easily seen in documents, photographs, maps and physical spaces. Some examples of facts are: Spanish colonial Franciscan priests, led by Junipero Serra, ultimately moved at least 100,000 indigenous people from forty or more tribes into 21 missions. The Mexican Plan de Iguala secularized the mission property and freed the Indians from their bonds to the missions. Between 1849-50 over 300,000 Americans migrated to California gold country. **Common beliefs** are often accepted as truth but are often a biased version of what happened. An example is that Indians disappeared because they lacked immunity to European disease during the mission period. Lands of Our Ancestor challenges social truths by telling the Chumash perspective. **Personal experiences** such as those found in journals, letters, and oral accounts of people who lived during that time. These accounts do not have to agree to be true. Understanding how each side felt and experienced the historical events is important. **Universal truths** help individuals or communities come to terms with an injustice. For example, all people want the freedom to choose how they live their lives. All parents want a better life for their children. Personal identity and communities are shaped by their connection to their environment. By acknowledging harm instead of erasing it, healing can occur.

Below are two examples of historical research used in Land of Our Ancestors to write scenes depicting daily life at the missions, forced labor, and punishment inflicted by the Spanish on the Indians. See if you can identify the four different types of truths.

Junipero Serra's mandate from the King of Spain was to educate the Indians of California and then release them. Instead, Serra took it upon himself to effectively imprison them for life and use the Native Americans as forced labor... The mission Indians, called neophytes by the friars, had terrible, sadistic punishments inflicted on them by the Franciscans... One distinguished visitor to Mission Carmel was shocked at the fetid squalor in which the Indians were forced to live. Bedraggled Indians, some in shackles and stocks, were being walked to a work site accompanied by guards who swung whips to ensure their staying together.

The sight, he wrote in his log, was no different than the slave plantations he'd visited in the Caribbean. He described the policies of the Franciscans toward the mission Indians as reprehensible, adding they were beating the Indians for violations that in Europe would be considered insignificant.

By far, one of the cruelest incidents was described in 1825 by Robert Forbes, the master of a New England trading ship. He visited Mission San Francisco and was shocked by the savagery of the friars. He took note of the "Christianizing Padres" who converted the Indians by sending gauchos and rancheros into the field to catch them with a lasso. He said the friars then branded the Indians with a hot branding iron shaped like a cross.

At both Mission San Gabriel and Mission San Luis Rey, the Indians faced the twisted wrath of Friar Jose Zalvidea. A visiting rancher noted the padre's penchant for punishment, including his cruelty toward women who suffered miscarriages. Instead of offering comfort, the friar ordered them to be lashed for 15 days, their heads shaved, and irons bolted around their ankles for 3 months. Each bereaved mother also had to stand every Sunday on the steps of the church holding a hideous painted wooden child in her arms.

Source: _A Cross of Thorns_ by Elias Castillo

Due to their "animal-like natures," California Indians often made mistakes or misbehaved even when they had been told the rules. Like good fathers everywhere, the padres believed in firm discipline and consequences; usually, this meant flogging, but sometimes other kinds of corporal punishment were used. In a long letter of complaint to the King of Spain, one South American Indian provided a catalog of Spanish punishments for Indians that included flogging, hanging upside down, and being put in stocks. Franciscan Fathers used these and other disciplinary actions to help "civilize" California Indians and turn them into good Christians and loyal Spanish subjects. These included those already mentioned, plus beating with a cudgel, whipping with a cat-o-nine tail, and hobbling with an ankle hobble.

Source: _Bad Indians_ by Deborah A. Miranda

Lands of our Ancestors Book One

The Spanish Mission Era

Historical Background

The Native American Perspective

The Chumash Indians have lived on California's Central Coast for at least 13,000 years. Their territory stretches from Malibu in the south to Morro Bay and San Luis Obispo in the north and from the Channel Islands in the west to the inland areas around Cuyama, California. Over time, the language of these autonomous groups evolved into eight different versions of the Chumash language, known as dialects. Another example of regional languages evolving from a root language can be found in Europe. Latin, spoken during the Greek and Roman empires, spread and evolved into Italian, Spanish, French, Portuguese, and English.

The Chumash way of life depended on the natural world around them. This world provided everything the people needed: food, clothing, shelter, medicine, tools, and weapons. Because they lived so close to nature, the Chumash had very detailed knowledge about the wild plants, animals, and minerals that they relied on.

They knew how to use more than 150 plants for food, medicine, and ceremonial applications. These included oak trees for acorns, chia seeds from sage plants, nuts, seeds, bulbs, roots, and leaves of many other plants. However, acorns were *the* most important plant food for the Chumash and most California Indians. Acorns are poisonous to humans unless ground into a fine meal, washed (leached) at least three times, and then cooked. This makes a filling, thick brown mush somewhat like oatmeal, often eaten with more flavorful foods like dried fish or venison (deer meat). Pine nuts were also an important food. Trips to pine tree forests at distant higher elevations were part of the Chumash annual food-gathering cycle.

They were skillful hunters of wild games such as deer, antelope, rabbits, birds, and seals. They also enjoyed a wide variety of fish and shellfish from the ocean and rivers in the area. Salmon of the Santa Ynez River was one of their favorites.

The Chumash home was built of Tule reeds spread over frames made of willow branches. This round half-dome house called an *ap* (op), included a small fire pit at the center with a small smoke hole in the roof. The sizes of these homes varied greatly depending on the size of the family living in one. A village was often made up of rows of aps. It included an enclosed area for religious activities, acorn storage facilities, a playing field for sporting games, and a sweat house where daily hot sweat baths were taken for cleansing and healing.

Their religious beliefs included an understanding of certain supernatural powers that resided in the natural world, including the sky world. Movements of the sun, moon, and stars revealed hidden meanings to the tribal spiritual leaders who keep an ever-watchful eye on the sky. These people were part of the twelve-member council called the *antap* (on top) that provided leadership and guidance to community members. Each major village had its council of twelve, which included the local village chief.

This way of life was developed and practiced for thousands of years until Spanish priests, soldiers, and settlers arrived in the 1700s.

NATIVE PEOPLE OF THIS PLACE

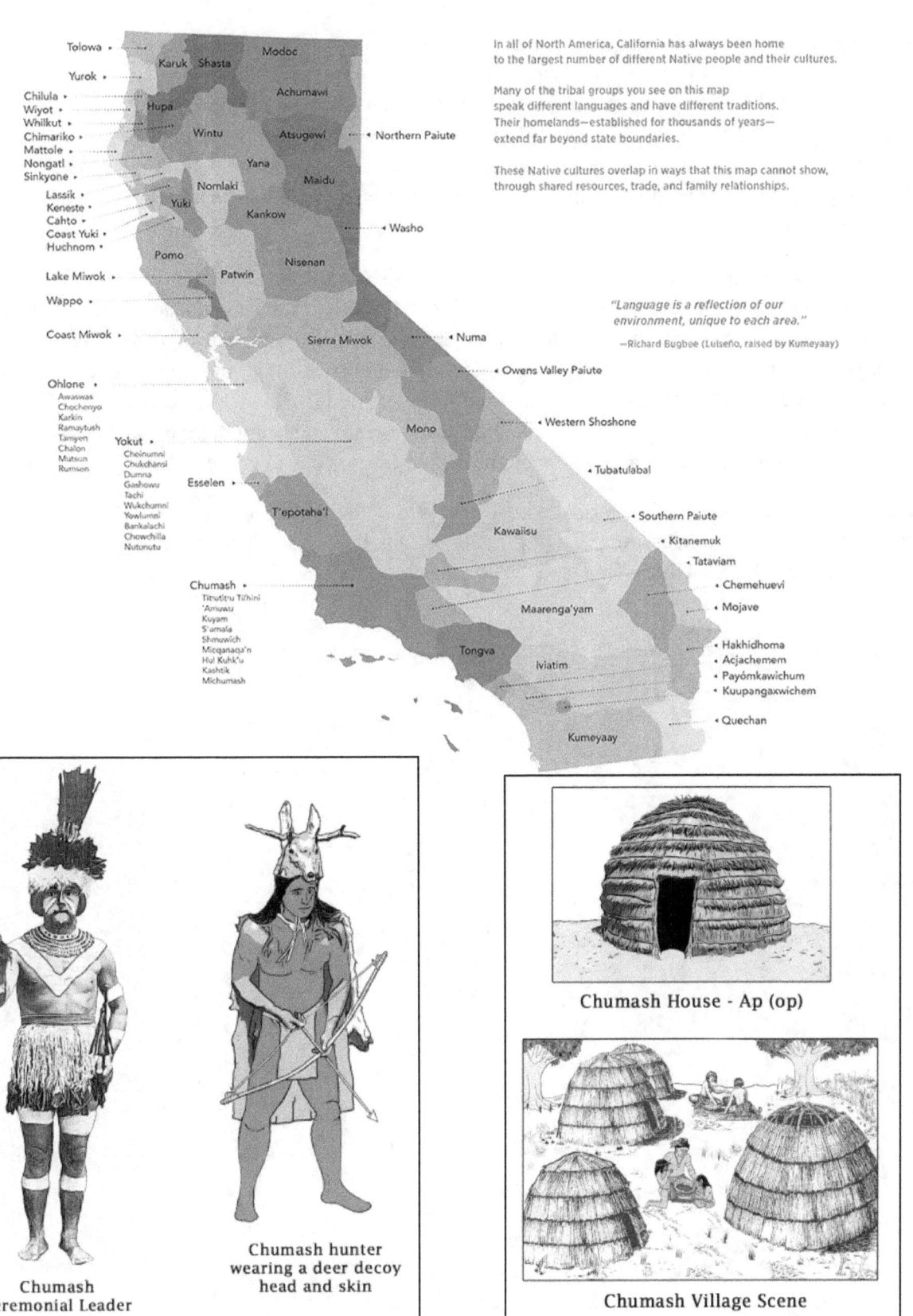

In all of North America, California has always been home to the largest number of different Native people and their cultures.

Many of the tribal groups you see on this map speak different languages and have different traditions. Their homelands—established for thousands of years—extend far beyond state boundaries.

These Native cultures overlap in ways that this map cannot show, through shared resources, trade, and family relationships.

"Language is a reflection of our environment, unique to each area."
—Richard Bugbee (Luiseño, raised by Kumeyaay)

Map labels:

Tolowa, Karuk, Shasta, Modoc, Yurok, Achumawi, Chilula, Wiyot, Whilkut, Hupa, Chimariko, Mattole, Wintu, Atsugewi, Northern Paiute, Nongatl, Sinkyone, Yana, Lassik, Nomlaki, Maidu, Keneste, Yuki, Cahto, Kankow, Coast Yuki, Huchnom, Washo, Pomo, Nisenan, Lake Miwok, Patwin, Wappo, Coast Miwok, Sierra Miwok, Numa, Ohlone (Awaswas, Chochenyo, Karkin, Ramaytush, Tamyen, Chalon, Mutsun, Rumsen), Owens Valley Paiute, Yokut (Cheinumni, Chukchansi, Dumna, Gashowu, Tachi, Wukchumni, Yowlumni, Bankalachi, Chowchilla, Nutunutu), Mono, Western Shoshone, Esselen, Tubatulabal, T'epotaha'l, Southern Paiute, Kawaiisu, Kitanemuk, Tataviam, Chumash (Titutitu Ti/hini, 'Amuwu, Kuyam, S'amala, Shmuwich, Micqanaqa'n, Hul Kuhk'u, Kashtik, Michumash), Chemehuevi, Mojave, Maarenga'yam, Hakhidhoma, Tongva, Acjachemem, Iviatim, Payómkawichum, Kuupangaxwichem, Quechan, Kumeyaay

Chumash Ceremonial Leader

Chumash hunter wearing a deer decoy head and skin

Chumash House - Ap (op)

Chumash Village Scene

The Spanish Perspective

Explorers sailing on Spanish ships visited the California coast a few times in the 1500s and 1600s, looking for gold and trade routes. It wasn't until 1769 that Gaspar de Portola led an expedition to the region to establish permanent settlements here. This was a combined religious and military effort to ensure that Spain had firm colonial control of the area. Franciscan priests were charged with the duty of creating Catholic missions to convert Indians to Christianity, and soldiers were assigned the duty of maintaining order within these communities. Their ultimate goal was to add more territory to the Spanish empire.

Starting in San Diego, twenty-one missions were established and operated, but these institutions were more like slave plantations than outposts of the Christian faith. Indians who came to the missions were forced to work daily to build all the buildings, raise and slaughter cattle, plant and harvest crops, prepare and cook food, weave cloth for clothing, and perform all the tasks needed to maintain a Spanish settlement. If Indians failed to do their work or tried to run away because of the way they were treated, soldiers on horseback were sent to capture them and bring them back. Then, the Indians were often beaten with whips as punishment or locked in shackles to prevent them from trying again.

Five missions were built in Chumash territory, and due to the spread of European diseases and abusive slave labor practices, the tribal population shrank by at least 80% during the sixty-year mission period. This was true of the Native American population all over the California region.

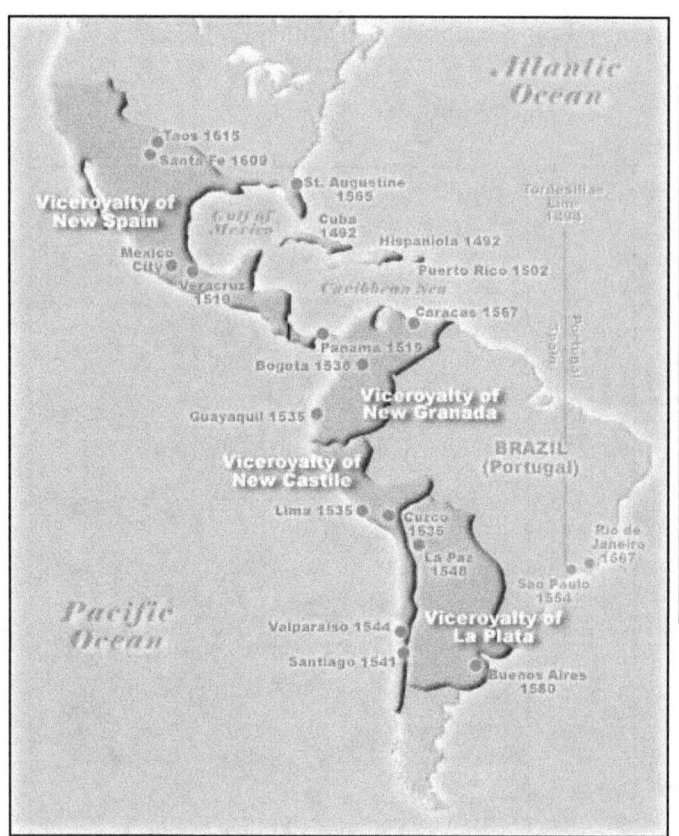

*Etching of Spanish Explorers and Indigenous People by Bertrand

For Further Reading

Blackburn, Thomas. December's Child: A book of Chumash Oral Narratives. University of California Press, Berkeley Press. 1975.

Bush Gibson, Karen. The Chumash, Seafarers of the Pacific Coast; Capstone Press, 2004.

California's Chumash Indians, A Project of the Santa Barbara Museum of Natural History; EZ Nature Books; 1992, Revised Edition 2002.

Castillo, Elias. A Cross of Thorns-The Enslavement of California's Indians by the Spanish Missions; Craven Street Books; 2015.

Fogel, Daniel. Junipero Serra, the Vatican, and Enslavement Theology; Ism Press; 1988.

Gamble, Lynn. The Chumash World at European Contact. University of California Press. 2008

Miranda, Deborah A. Bad Indians: A Tribal Memoir; Heyday, 2013.

Resendez, Andres. The Other Slavery-The Uncovered Story of Indian Enslavement in America; Houghton Mifflin Harcourt; 2016.

"The Samala People" (DVD); produced by the Santa Ynez Band of Chumash Indians; Available from the tribe's Culture Department; 805-688-7997.

Samala-English Dictionary-A Guide to the Samala Language of the Ineseno Chumash People; Santa Ynez Band of Chumash Indians with Richard Applegate, PhD; 2007.

Website: www.sbnature.org/research/anthro/chumash/intro.htm (Chumash section of the Santa Barbara Museum of Natural History's website)

Website: www.santaynezchumash.org/history.html (The Santa Ynez Band of Chumash Indians official website)

Website: http:// www.whenturtlesfly.blogspot.com - Deborah Miranda's blog on California Indians and the Native experience in the missions.

Book 1 Student Worksheets

Lands of Our Ancestors Book 1, Chapter 1

1. Complete the Venn diagram below for the two main characters Kilik and Tuhuy. Compare and contrast the boys' personalities, skills, goals, and relationships.

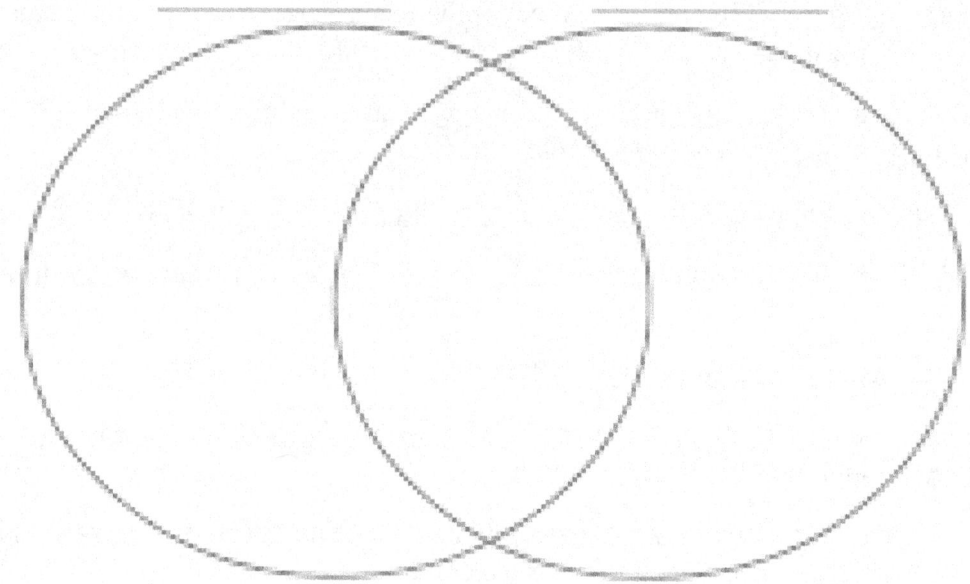

2. What are three facts about the Place of River Turtles that describe how the Chumash are connected to the earth?

3. Match the Chumash names with the characters:

___ Yol

___ Solomol   a. Tuhuy's father 'To Lift Up'

___ Wonono   b. Tuhuy's mother 'Bluebird'

___ Stuk   c. Kilik's father 'Straight Arrow'

___ Salapay   d. Kilik's mother 'Small Owl'

                         e. Kilik's sister 'Ladybug'

Lands of Our Ancestors Book 1, Chapter 2

1. Without a formal school or a written language, how do Chumash children learn the skills and knowledge they need to become contributing members of the village community? Who teaches Kilik and Tuhuy?

2. How could children maintain the Chumash culture if the elders suddenly disappeared?

3. How do you learn best? Reading, listening, watching, doing on your own, doing with a teacher?

4. What do the Chumash think about the double halos around the moon?

Lands of Our Ancestors Book 1, Chapter 3

1. The Chumash believed that the Sky People made them protectors and stewards of the land. How is stewardship demonstrated in Kilik's first hunt with his father?

Before . . .

During . . .

After . . .

2. The goal of colonization is not military conquest. The mission of the missions was to convert the land into farms and the people into citizens and Catholics. What steps were taken during the first meeting towards colonization?

Present themselves as friendly, not threatening . . .

Communicate trust . . .

Promise a better life . . .

Lands of Our Ancestors Book 1, Chapter 4

1. The priest extends an invitation to visit the mission. The Chumash chief talks options over with the elders. What might be some of the benefits of going to the mission? How can they protect themselves and resist being taken over by this powerful new group of people?

We Should Visit the Mission Because . . .	We Should Resist Oppression By . . .

2. When it comes to language, who has an advantage and who has a disadvantage? Why?

3. How is conversion already happening at the camp?

    a.   Converting the land . . .

    b.   Converting the people . . .

4. Describe three ways the Spanish got the Chumash to stay on the mission.

    1.

    2.

    3.

Lands of Our Ancestors Book 1, Chapter 5

1. Explain how the following helped the Spanish colonize the Indians.

Separate sleeping quarters	
Required clothing	
Take their weapons	
Baptism	

2. Even if you wanted to, why might you choose not to leave?

3. What do Kilik, Solomol, and Salapay finally realize on the second morning in camp?

Lands of Our Ancestors Book 1, Chapter 6

1. Describe how the bells, hard labor, and food are used to enslave the Indians.

2. How do jobs influence our sense of personal identity?

2. What advice does the translator give to Kilik and Tuhuy?

"Never say your . . .

"Just keep . . .

"Don't try to . . .

Lands of Our Ancestors Book 1, Chapter 7

1. It was often too dangerous to fight, run away, or question the padre's authority.

Which of the following was *not* a common punishment at the missions?

_____ Kicked out of the mission and sent back to the village.

_____ Sent to a different mission further away from family and tribe.

_____ Less food, washing mouth with soap, and harder work.

_____ Sent to church to pray all day with the priest.

_____ Whipped, put in shackles, hobbled, or beaten by soldiers.

2. What are some things Kilik and his family do to resist the changes imposed on their culture in the mission system?

3. Fill in the blanks for the rules of the mission.

Only allowed to speak _____ and read the _____.

Worshipping, singing and dancing _____ religion is forbidden.

Once baptized Indians are forbidden to _____ without priest permission.

Separate sleeping quarters from _____ is required.

Must wear _____and shoes provided by the priests at all times.

When the church bells ring all Indians have to _____.

Lands of Our Ancestors Book 1, Chapter 8

1. Describe the role of a trustee at the mission. Who are they, what is their job, and how are they paid/rewarded?

2. Site four examples from this chapter explaining why Indians didn't leave the missions, even if they were unhappy.

3. Was Father Espíritu a good or bad man? Support your comments with examples from the story.

4. What advantages do Kilik and Tuhuy have when working as Father Espíritu's assistants? What important information do they learn?

Lands of Our Ancestors Book 1, Chapter 9

1. Compare and contrast the motives of Father Espíritu, Father Fiero, and Captain Castigar regarding "the small vacation".

They all wanted:		
Father Espiritu wanted	Father Fiero wanted	Captain Castigar wanted

2. List two ways the soldiers disrespected the Indians during the day away from the mission.

3. What does the village elder tell Solomol and Salapay when they visit the Place of the River Turtles? How are they impacted by the missions, too?

Lands of Our Ancestors Book 1, Chapter 10

1. After two years, what evidence do the priest and soldiers have to prove that the mission successfully converted the land into Spanish-style farms and ranches?

What evidence proves they have converted the people into obedient Spanish peasant farmers?

2. After two years, describe the cost of this success.

Indian lands and resources . . .

Indian health . . .

Indian traditional culture . . .

Priest's feelings about the loss of Indian lives . . .

3. How would you describe the relationship between Kilik and Tuhuy after two years in the mission?

4. Discuss what some Chumash leaders do secretly and its importance.

Lands of Our Ancestors Book 1, Chapter 11

1. Complete the diagram to show the important trade relationship between the missions and Mexico. (Which items traveled from the missions to Mexico? Which items flowed from Mexico to the missions?

Items: Cowhide, wool blankets, fancy objects, mail, chocolate, world news, grains, raw metal, currency, credit reports.

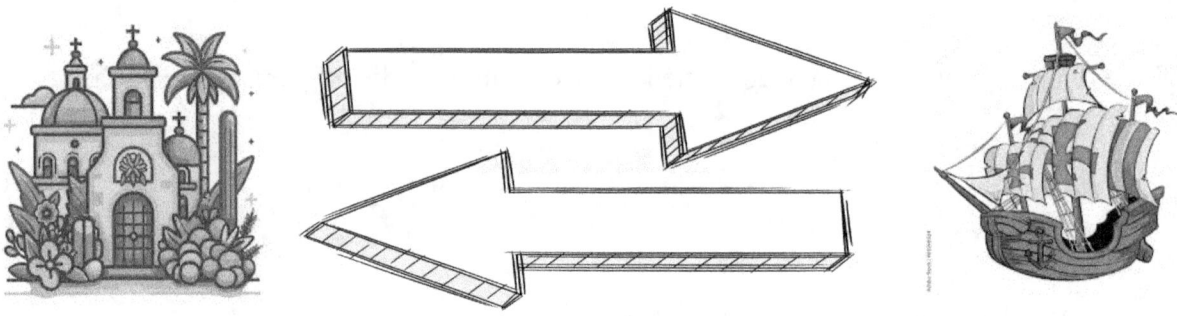

2. Why was it so important for the Spanish to keep news of Indian revolts a secret?

Lands of Our Ancestors Book 1, Chapter 12

1. How does news travel between the missions for the Indians?

2. When will the Indian attack happen? How long do the Indians have to prepare?

3. Even though Solomol doesn't think the Indians will beat the Spanish, what does he hope the revolt will accomplish?

4. How does Father Espíritu demonstrate he is an ally?

Lands of Our Ancestors Book 1, Chapter 13

1. Write a tweet describing the morning of the Summer Solstice.

2. Several priests, like Father Espíritu, chose to be allies and help the Native Californians. Based on the decision tree below, was he a brave man?

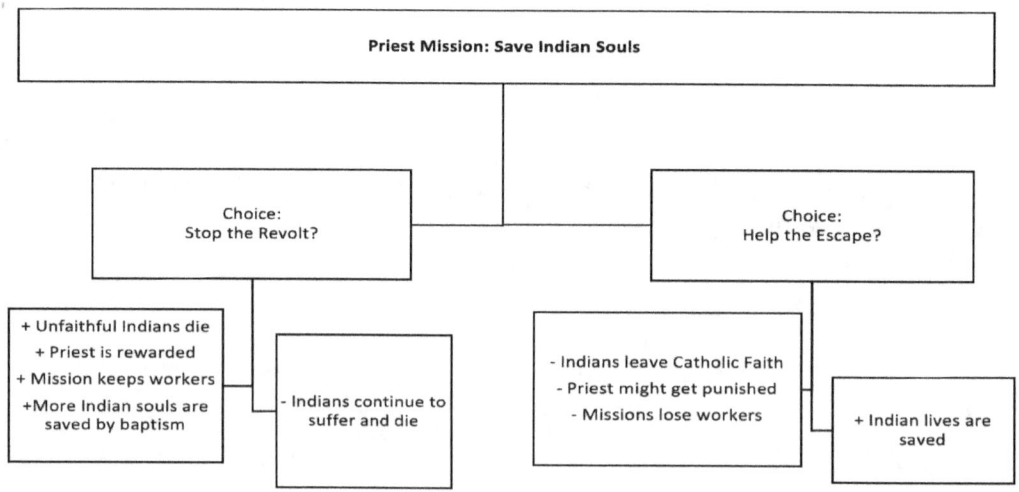

Chapter 13 continued:

3. Complete the decision tree below explaining why the Father didn't do more.

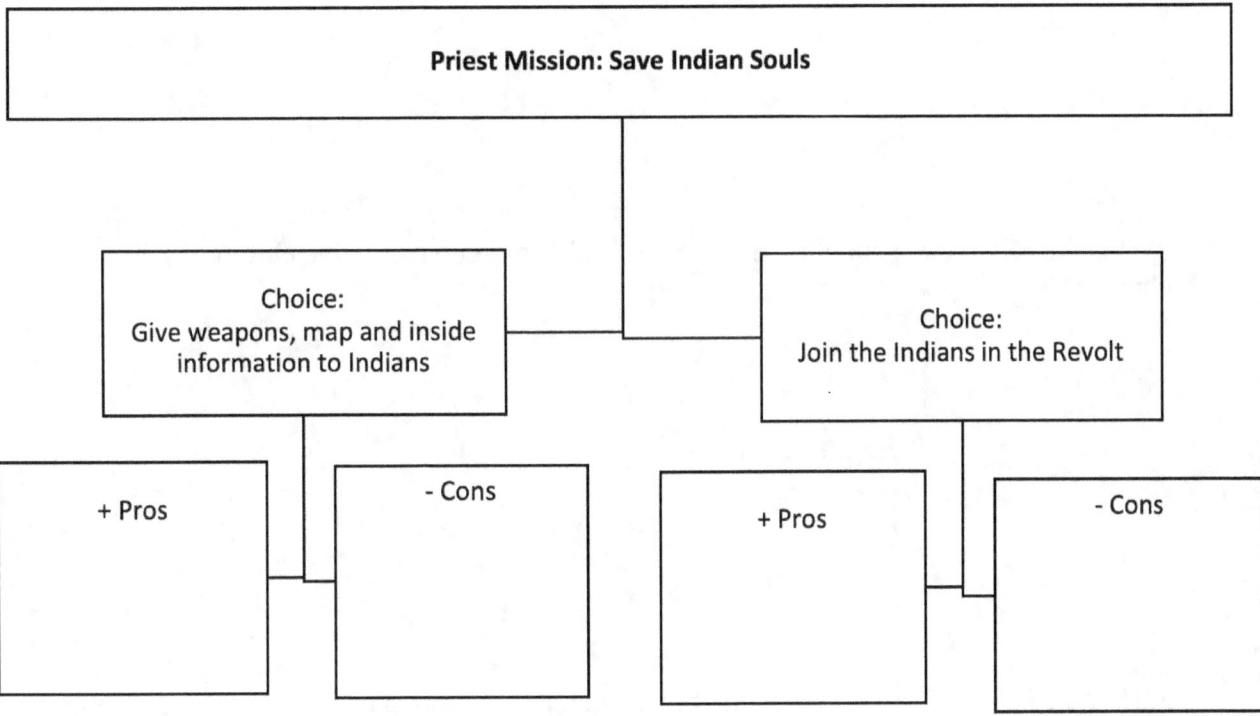

Priest Mission: Save Indian Souls

Choice:
Give weapons, map and inside information to Indians

Choice:
Join the Indians in the Revolt

+ Pros

- Cons

+ Pros

- Cons

Lands of Our Ancestors Book 1, Chapter 14

1. What might have happened if Father Espíritu had not been waiting at the chapel with the keys to the door?

2. How do Kilik and Tuhuy use their special skills to keep the native children safe in the chapel?

3. If you could speak to Solomol and Salapay on the afternoon of the revolt, what would you tell them?

Lands of Our Ancestors Book 1, Chapter 15

1. What great responsibility do Kilik and Tuhuy accept?

2. List the skills and knowledge Kilik learned from his father to escape to Sacred Mountain.

3. Why *didn't* Solomol and Salapay help everyone escape through the secret door?

Lands of Our Ancestors Book 1, Chapter 16

1. What obstacles do Kilik, Tuhuy, and the native children encounter in the wilderness?

2. How did their parent's lessons about nature impact the children's escape from the soldiers and survival in the wilderness?

3. Who do you think will survive, the children in the wilderness or the adults in the mission?

Book 1 Worksheet Answer Keys

Chapter 1 Answer Key
1. Kilik is twelve years old. His name means "Sparrow Hawk". He is confident, determined, athletic, and a leader. Kilik is eager to use hunting skills to bring food to the village.

Tuhuy is eleven years old. His name means "Rain". He is a "thinker" and is determined to improve his skills, although he does not believe he will ever be as skilled as Kilik.

Kilik and Tuhuy are cousins *and* best friends who are always together. They are kind, obedient, and respectful to their families and elders. They work together, each using their special abilities to complete a task or solve a problem.

2. Facts about the Place of the River Turtle.
- Hutash, the yearly harvest festival, celebrates Mother Earth.
- Homes are made of tule reeds.
- They are named after nature.
- Dances, songs, and stories are about nature.
- Food, like acorns and deer, are found close by to the river.

3. Kilik and Tuhuy are cousins.

  b   Yol   a.Tuhuy's father 'To Lift Up'

  c   Solomol   b.Tuhuy's mother 'Bluebird'

                                  c.Kilik's father 'Straight Arrow'

  d   Wonono   d. Kilik's mother 'Small Owl'

  e   Stuk   e. Kilik's sister 'Ladybug'

  a   Salapay

Chapter 2 Answer Key
1. Children learn skills from their elders by seeing, hearing, and doing. The hoop-and-pole game helps boys develop their hunting skills. Kilik is determined to have sharp skills for his first hunt. Kilik's father teaches him the area's important landmarks, trails, place names, and geography. Kilik needs to know this information because one day, he will hunt alone, and he needs to understand the land.

2. Without the elders, the village would quickly collapse because the people do not have any written language to learn from.

3.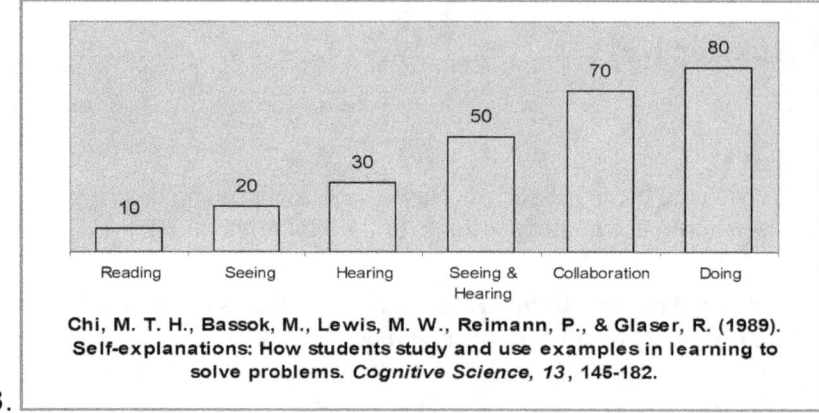

Chi, M. T. H., Bassok, M., Lewis, M. W., Reimann, P., & Glaser, R. (1989). Self-explanations: How students study and use examples in learning to solve problems. *Cognitive Science, 13*, 145-182.

4. The double halos predict a drastic change in the lives of the Chumash people. Evidence from the story: A hunter tells Solomol that strange people wearing odd clothing and speaking an odd language who seem to have more powers than the Chumash leaders have been seen on the lands of the Chumash and in the south. These strange people are Spanish soldiers and priests who have come to take the land of the Chumash people.

Chapter 3 Answer Key

1. Before praying to Grandfather Sun, camouflage themselves with deerskin. While following animal trails, prayer of thanks to the deer. After Kilik has become a man, gets a talisman necklace of the protector.

2. Nonthreatening by putting priests in front of soldiers. Communicate trust with Indian translators. Promise a better life by showing their powerful weapons and horses, offering to share food and their powerful knowledge.

Chapter 4 Answer Key

1. Benefits: Trade, knowledge of their power, and better understanding of the potential threat. Resistance: Send only the strongest protectors, take their weapons, and don't stay long.

2. Europeans all speak Spanish. Indians speak many different languages and dialects. This language barrier keeps the Indians isolated from each other.

3. Converting the land: oak trees turned into firewood and lumber. Livestock destroying vegetation. Converting the people: eat different food and forced to plow fields and build adobe by soldiers.

4. The priests and soldiers continue to promise new skills, their lives will improve, and they will be paid for their work. The soldiers surround the native people to keep them in the camp. The people of the Place of the River Turtles are unaware that when they enter the camp, they will be captive, unable to leave.

Chapter 5 Answer Key

1. **Separated** to begin to break down the family groups. This gives the priests and soldiers control and prevents the native people from leaving if family members are in unknown locations in the camp. (Accept additional reasonable answers.) Wear European **clothing** to change how the natives live. Remove the native men's **weapons** while they sleep so they cannot fight or escape. The **translator tells the men the baptism message** is: "Man-in-sky has delivered you to us. And here you and our people will stay." The priest then gives the native people Spanish names.

2. They might stay to be with their family and friends. They might not know how to survive totally on their own. They might not want to lead soldiers back to their village.

3. In the morning, Kilik, Solomol, and Salapay finally realize they will not leave the camp. They are not guests; they are captives.

Chapter 6 Answer Key

1. Instead of following the natural time of the sun and seasons, the Indians' lives are now controlled by mission bells. The bells keep the people moving from task to task in a regimented way: lining up, waiting, working, eating, and sleeping. The strange food kept the native people hungry and poorly nourished. The hard physical labor kept people tired. Tired, hungry people are less likely to fight the soldiers or try to escape.

2. Jobs influence identity, pride, and purpose. Consider the difference between Kilik after his first hunt and after his first day of making Adobe bricks.

3. "Don't mention Chumash names in front of priests."
"Keep busy to avoid trouble."
"Don't try to run away, and you will be captured and punished."

Chapter 7 Answer Key

1. Kicked out of the mission and sent back to the village. Sent to church to pray all day with the priest.

2. Kilik and his family quietly break the rules at mealtime so they can speak their native language, remember who they are and where they come from, and keep hope alive.

3. Fill in the blanks for the rules of the mission.

Only allowed to speak _Spanish_ and read the _Bible._

Worshipping, singing, and dancing _Native_ religion is forbidden.

Once baptized, Indians are forbidden to _leave_ without priest permission.

Separate sleeping quarters from _family, men/women_ is required.

Must wear _mission clothing_ and shoes provided by the priests at all times.

When the church bells ring, all Indians have to _report to church._

Chapter 8 Answer Key

1. The trustees are Indians who have been at the mission for a long time and speak Spanish well. The padres choose them. The trustees make sure the Indians follow the rules and report any problems or rule-breaking to the padres and soldiers. If the trustee does not do his job, he and his family will be punished.

2. Site four examples from this chapter explaining why Indians didn't leave the missions, even if they were unhappy.

   - Saw other Indians fail and get punished.
   - Too tired and depressed to leave.
   - Don't want to bring trouble to their village.
   - Don't want to leave family behind at the mission.
   - Trustees tell the soldiers and padres so the escape plan fails.

3. Was Father Espíritu a good or bad man? Support your comments with examples from the story.

Opinions about Father Espíritu will vary but should be supported by examples from the text. Father Espíritu wants to convert the Indians but feels they should not be harshly punished. He is a much kinder man than Father Fiero. Examples from the text:

• Father Espíritu thinks Father Fiero treats the Indians too cruelly. He confronts Father Fiero and says he will write a complaint letter to the head of the Missions in Mexico City.

• When Salapay and Solomol are flogged, Father Espíritu wants to give them medicine for their wounds, but Fiero won't let him.

• Father Espíritu feels sorry for Kilik's and Tuhuy's fathers and offers them jobs as his assistants. He admits to them that Father Fiero's punishments are too harsh.

4. When Kilik and Tuhuy begin working for Father Espíritu, they no longer have to do the hard work of making adobe bricks or working in the fields in the hot sun. They also have the opportunity to overhear conversations between the priests and gather information to share with other native people in the mission. Kilik and Tuhuy learn that originally, the native people would be released from the Mission when they became "civilized."

Chapter 9 Answer Key

1. Father Espíritu is sympathetic to the Indians after the flogging, and wants to raise their spirits. Father Fiero wants the Indians to start working and producing again. Father Espíritu convinces him that the day away from the mission will help. Captain Castigar wants to show the native people that their village is abandoned and they don't have homes to return to. This reinforces his control over the Indians and their feeling of helplessness.

2. The soldiers are disrespectful to the Indians on the day of their trip away from the mission in these ways:
   a. The soldiers eat and gorge themselves on the gathered and cooked food prepared by the Indian women. The Indians must eat whatever is left.
   b. Captain Castigar and the soldiers do not learn the Chumash language. Captain Castigar refers to the native language as "gibberish".
   c. When the Chumash visit their village, Captain Castigar is "smug" and seems happy to see the village in ruins and abandoned.
   d. The village elder they meet is left without food or help.

3. The village elder tells Solomol and Salapay that the Indians who have escaped from the missions are hiding at the base of Sacred Mountain. The missions affected all the native people, those

taken captive, and those left behind. People not taken to the mission were often the old ones. They could not provide for themselves and were left alone in the village. These people became sick, starved, and died. Those who escaped the missions had to stay in hiding, not to be captured; they were not completely free.

Chapter 10 Answer Key

1. Success! The mission's buildings are completed, and crops, cattle, and products for sale and trade are being made. Indians have learned Spanish, new jobs, and many have been baptized. Many of the villages have been abandoned and the Indians have moved onto the mission. Most are following the rules.
2. The Cost! Enslaved Indians have lost tribal lands that connected them to their way of life. They have lost many lives, and survivors are malnourished and sick. Death, isolation, and disconnected from each other and their land, much of the Indian culture has been lost.
   a. Priests demonstrated their feelings about the loss of Indians.
   b. "Most of those who died were unceremoniously placed in unmarked graves."
   c. "…a padre marked down the name of the deceased and the date of his death in a big book, but that was all."
   d. "…these departed Indians were gone and forgotten by the Spaniards."
3. Kilik and Tuhuy's relationship remains close and grows stronger through their shared difficult experiences. They continue to support and protect each other, help each other stay positive, and make games out of their work to avoid boredom.
4. The Chumash leaders continue to speak their language and mark traditional cycles of time the Chumash way. They are preserving the Chumash culture for future generations.

Chapter 11 Answer Key

1. Missions EXPORT: Cowhide, wool blankets, mail, grains, credit reports.
Spain EXPORTS: Fancy objects (tools, church art), mail, chocolate, raw metal, world news, currency.

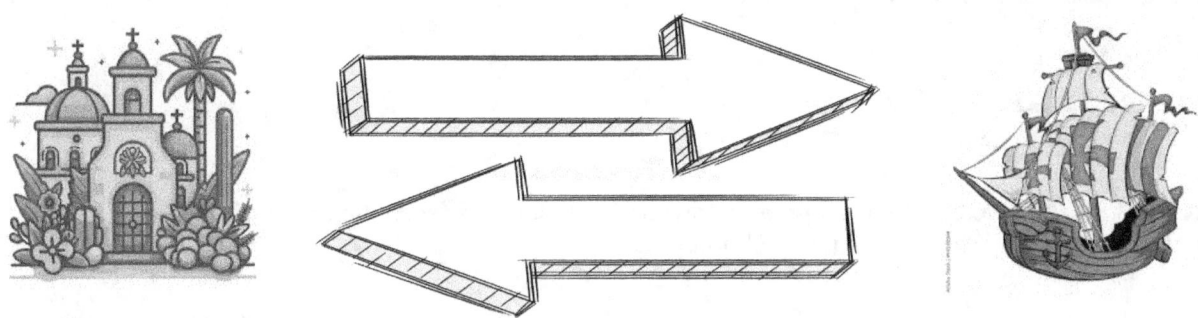

2. The Spaniards kept revolts secret so the news wouldn't inform and inspire others. It was important because the Indians outnumbered the Spanish, and reinforcements were far away.

Chapter 12 Answer Key

1. The Indians traveling with the Spanish pass messages between the missions.
2. The attack will happen on the Summer Solstice in the early morning while the soldiers eat breakfast. The Indians living in the mission have one week to prepare.
3. Solomol fights to provide a successful escape for the children. He realizes that the children must escape for the Chumash people to survive. Solomol is not confident that the revolt will be successful. He says, "If the rebellion fails, the future of the Chumash people is the younger generation." He also knows that the soldiers' weapons are more powerful than the Indians' bows and arrows.
4. Father Espíritu gives Kilik and Tuhuy medical supplies and a burlap bag of "traveling food." He also tells the boys that he doesn't approve of the mission's treatment of the Indians.

Chapter 13 Answer Key

1. Events on the morning of the Summer Solstice:
   - The Indians take weapons from the storage room and hide them.
   - Attacking Indians charge the mission.
   - Children led by Kilik and Tuhuy run to safety in the chapel.
   - Reynaldo is sent to the Presidio for help for the soldiers.
   - The fighting begins between the soldiers and Indians.

   The mood in the mission that morning is tense, anxious, fearful, angry, and possibly hopeful.

2. Opinions about Father Espiritu's bravery may vary.

3. Accept reasonable, thoughtful replies.

Chapter 14 Answer Key

2. Answers will vary.

3. Kilik uses his coordination and running skills to retrieve the burlap bag of food for the children. Tuhuy uses his problem-solving skills (thinking skills) to devise a lock for the chapel doors.

4. Accept reasonable answers.

Chapter 15 Answer Key

1. Kilik and Tuhuy must lead.

2. Kilik skills: knowledge of the geography, traveling without being seen, hunting animals, foraging plants, making fire, building shelter, defending children.

3. The adults stay at the mission and fight, causing a distraction so the children can escape. Everyone would have been too obvious. A large group moves slowly and would be easy for soldiers to track.

Chapter 16 Answer Key

1. Obstacles: difficult, slow walking off the trails, rain, hunger, fear of capture by soldiers, fatigue, cold, and broken-down shelters for sleeping. (Accept other reasonable answers.)

2. Understanding of nature: He finds animal trails for safety and uses tall grass to hide in. He recognizes landmarks such as Mother Oak to guide his way. Kilik uses the sounds of the horses' hooves and the flock of birds as warnings to hide. He knows what resources to use to make fire and find food. He understands how to find his direction to travel. He must go to a high point (Shrine Mountain).

3. Answers will vary.

Class Discussion Questions

Directions: Write one on the board for students to do a quick response at the beginning of class.

Identity

1. What experiences help you feel confident about your identity?
2. What and who shapes the personality of a child as they grow into an adult?

Community

1. Think about a community you belong to. How do the activities, common interests, and beliefs bind you together?
2. How do people's sense of community tie into their shared space?

Systems of Control

1. How does being separated from your community impact your sense of identity?
2. What would you do in a situation where you didn't speak the language?

Conflict & Resistance

1. Why is it hard to go against the dominant culture, the status quo, the authority?
2. Is it easier for someone on 'the inside' to resist? What consequences do they face for helping out a friend who is being oppressed?

Resilience

1. What does the phrase "existence is resistance" mean to you?
2. How do you continue your heritage in new and valuable ways?

Student Projects

The Bonds of Storytelling (ES 1)

Native Americans use oral storytelling rather than written language. At gathering ceremonies, people bond by listening to the same histories, legends, and traditions until everyone knows them by heart. That process forms their common history, the communities' shared identity, and what it means to be a member of this tribe.

Individually, elders pass on their skills and knowledge to the next generation. Societies with an oral tradition need more than good storytellers. They also depend on young people being good listeners, respecting the wisdom of their elders, and remembering what they have learned. This forms another critical bond between generations. It creates a continuity that runs through the generations for thousands of years.

Directions: Interview an elder in your community or family. Find out about a meaningful lesson they learned when they were young that has helped them their whole lives. It can be advice or an experience, good or bad, personal or something everyone went through.

Retell that story to the class:
Make it mysterious, funny, or scary as long as it's memorable for your audience.
Give a detailed description of the characters, including names, what they looked like, and personalities.

Describe the community they belonged to; generation, place, social group, rich or poor.
The message, or takeaway lesson, should be universal to help anyone listening.

Colonial Rules (ES 3, ES 4)

Europeans colonized much of the world during the 1600s-1700s. Taking control of the land through a military assault was not strategically possible. The land and population were too big to conquer that way. Instead, European success relied on systems that oppressed and subdued the Indigenous people. Two important systems used by Spain were the Casta System and the Mission System.

By the time Father Junipero Serra arrived in California, Spain had ruled over most of Latin America for 250 years with the help of hundreds of missions built and operated by the Catholic Church.

Directions:

Use the interactive map from www.ourworldindata.org to find a different European colony outside the Americas.

URL: https://ourworldindata.org/grapher/european-overseas-colonies-and-their-colonizers?time=1691

Create a chart that compares the California mission system with the systems and rules in the other colony you picked.

	California 'New Spain'	Other Colony
Colonizer	Spain (1769-1835)	
Who had property rights, and who didn't?		
Who set wages and prices?		
What was the role of the church in colonizing?		
Was everyone equal in the eyes of the law?		
Who had the power to settle complaints or disputes?		
What rules kept Europeans in positions of power?		

Legacy of California Missions (ES 3, ES4)

Generational trauma, also called intergenerational trauma, is how the psychological effects of traumatic events experienced by one generation are passed down to the next generations. Even if the child did not directly experience the original trauma; the pain their parents suffered is passed on through harmful family dynamics and negative coping mechanisms.

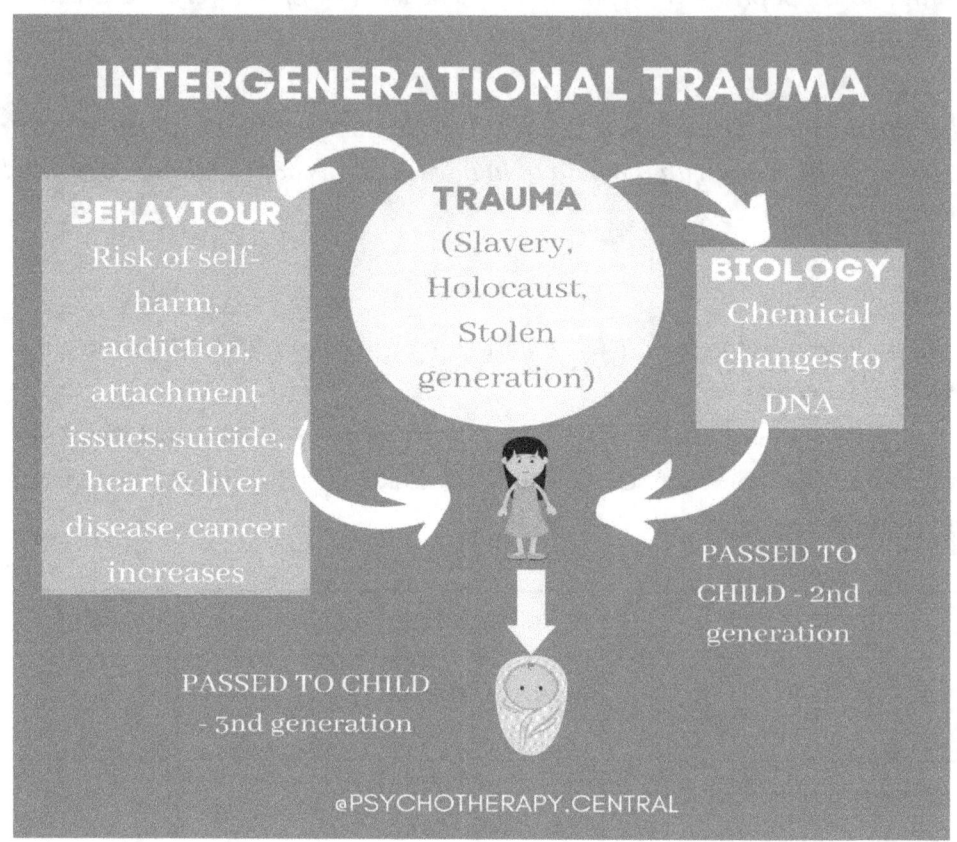

Directions:

Create two posters. The first illustrates the intergenerational trauma of California Native Americans, and the second illustrates ways to heal from intergenerational trauma.

Include five facts, four pictures, three quotes, two charts, and one amazing title. (Be sure to cite your sources on the back)

Correcting History

Read Deborah Miranda's 2017 article in Huffington Post "Lying to Children About the California Missions and the Indians".

URL: https://www.huffpost.com/entry/lying-to-children-about-t_b_6924346

What are some of the common stereotypes that need to be corrected?

Next, review the www.missionscalifornia.com, hosted by the California Missions Resource Center. Identify biased language, stereotypes and missing information.

Create a presentation that shows how you would edit this website. You can either print things out and make a science board or do screenshots and make a PowerPoint. Show us the before and then the after that gives a more balanced and accurate account of history.

Lands of our Ancestors Book Two

The Mexican Rancho Period

Historical Summary

Indian Perspective

This work of historical fiction depicts what might have happened to California Native Americans during the Mexican rancho era 1822-1846. Although the characters and their stories are fictional, the events, culture, and socio-political climate are based on historical facts. The Mexican Rancho period was a second wave of colonization. It continued to destroy Native American peoples, communities, and cultures across California.

After ten years of fighting, Mexico finally won independence from Spain in 1821 which signaled the end of the mission era. There was political chaos for several decades afterwards as factions within the new government fought for control. The most serious mission uprisings occurred during this politically chaotic time.

Contributing to the decline of the missions was the loss of free Indian labor. In 1821, the population of baptized Indians (neophytes) at the missions peaked at 21,000, but by 1834, less than 16,000 remained. Conditions had grown intolerable as thousands of Indians died from disease. There were no more local Indian villages to recruit replacement workers. Those that remained were increasingly overworked, faced growing abuse from soldiers, and with reduced yield were often underfed. Consequently, many chose to run away.

In 1833, the Mexican government passed a law secularizing the missions. The law required the missions to free the Indians and give them their land back. Livestock, equipment, and seeds previously belonging to the missions were also supposed to be supplied to the freed neophytes. However, most of the land and property was taken by the Californios who drove off the Indians. Without their own land to support themselves, some moved to local pueblos where they found work alongside former soldiers and Mestizo tradesmen. Others moved to California's interior to live with relatives or fellow tribesmen. Most ex-neophytes had no choice but to find work on the Californios ranchos doing essentially the same jobs they had performed at the missions.

While the jobs were the same, Indian lives were different during the Mexican rancho period. Unlike the mission priests, the ranchero owners didn't care how the Indians lived their lives. Some rancheros allowed families and communities to stay together and practice their traditional lifestyle as long as it didn't interfere with their work. While they had political and social freedom, economically the Indians were still trapped. Rancheros kept their Indian workers indebted to them by paying them 'in kind' with food, housing, and sometimes liquor. Bound to the rancho by **peonage**, the Native Americans were treated as slaves. The Native Americans who worked on the ranchos died at twice the rate that of southern slaves.

California Indians were economically important to the successful operation of the ranchos, as reflected in a statement made by a prominent ranchero:

Many of the rich men of the country had from twenty to sixty Indian servants whom they dressed and fed.... Indians tilled our soil, pastured our cattle, sheared our sheep, cut our lumber, built our houses, paddled our boats, made tiles for our homes, ground our grain, slaughtered our cattle, dressed their hides for the market, and made our unburnt bricks; In contrast, the Indian women made excellent servants, cared for our children, made every one of our meals...

Salvador Vallejo in Cook 1943b:51

During this era resistance grew from independent Indians living in the interior. The Indian offensive from the Central Valley reached a peak in 1845. Raids on horse herds increased throughout the mission, rancho and the American eras. The enormous herds of horses were tempting targets because they were easier to drive off than cattle. Horses were used for transportation and replaced food sources wiped out by Spanish and Mexican settlements. This dietary change saved entire villages from starvation. The military and rancheros began raiding interior Indian groups to catch horse thieves and enslave more laborers. Formerly peaceful, sedentary, localized groups grew more aggressive, nomadic and coordinated. In fact, the Indian raids on coastal settlements became such a threat that the Mexican government planned to establish a military border police and erect a fort at Pacheco Pass.

For example, in 1837 José Marí Amador, a wealthy rancher, led a party of civilians, soldiers, and Indian auxiliaries on an expedition into the San Joaquin Valley, where they encountered a group of about 200 suspected wrongdoers, including 100 or so ex-neophytes. Amador wrote in his journal; *"invited the wild Indians and their Christian companions to come and have a feast."* When the Indians came into the Mexican camp, armed members of the expedition who had been in hiding surrounded the Indians and quickly subdued them. Amador then separated the Christian Indians and, as he wrote,

"At every half-mile or mile, we put six of them on their knees, making them understand that they were about to die. Each one was shot with four arrows, two in front and two in the back. Those who refused to die immediately were killed with spears. On the road, they were killed in this manner: the 100 Christians."

Later, Amador decided to execute the unconverted prisoners after he first baptized them.

"I ordered Nazario Galindo to take a water bottle, and I took another. He began at one part of the crowd and I at another. We baptized all the Indians, and afterward, they were shot in the back. At the first volley, 70 fell dead. I doubled the charge for the 30 who remained, and they all fell."

The devastating effects of European diseases originating in the mission era did not stop during the Mexican era. They were even more devastating to the Central Valley Indians than military expeditions. In the early 1830s, Hudson's Bay Company trappers passed through the Great Valley, introducing malaria into the marshy interior lowlands. The disease killed an estimated 20,000 Indians and remained endemic after that. By the end of the Mexican occupation, the total Native population of California had been reduced to about 100,000 persons.

Mexican Ranchero Perspective

The King of Spain gave each mission about 1,000,000 acres (1,500 square miles). However, between 1784 and 1821, he only gave 30 land concessions, mostly to retired soldiers. Soldiers, rancheros, farmers, and the growing elite families of colonial New Spain wanted the rich lands that the missions controlled. "Tierra y Libertad!" (land and liberty) were a major reason for the Mexican Revolution. After they won the revolution, the Mexican government feared the missions would remain loyal to the Pope and the Catholic Church in Spain.

In August 1833, the government passed the **Secularization Acts** to break up the Church's monopoly on the land. The missions were only left with the church, priest's quarters, and priest's garden. The army guards posted at each Mission were dismissed and the government sold mission property as **Land grants** ranging in size from 4,500 to 50,000 acres. In the end about 800 elite Californio families who, with the help of their friends in power, got almost all of the 270 land grants between 1833 and 1846. The "rancheros" (rancho owners) patterned themselves after the landed gentry of colonial New Spain. The grantee could not initially subdivide or rent the land. It had to be used for grazing or cultivation. So, like the missions before them, the ranchos produced hides for the world leather market and relied on Indian labor.

Major Dates

1810-1821	Mexican Revolution. Spanish stop sending resupply ships to Alta California.
1820s	Indian revolts and raids increase across mission system
1826	The Mexican constitution frees mission Indians
1833	Secularization Acts breaks up the mission's land monopoly. Flu epidemic across California kills thousands of Indians.
1833-1846	270 land grants are issued to 800 Californio rancho elite families.
1844	Smallpox outbreak across California kills thousands of Indians.

Images of Mexican Rancho Life

ABOVE: Example of a two story Mexican Rancho house similar to the one described in Lands of our Ancestors Book Two.
-Petaluma Adobe State Historic Park

LEFT: Example of Mexican Rancho map that shows the boundary lines of neighboring ranchos. This map shows ranchos in Alameda County near Hayward.
-Hayward Area Historical Society

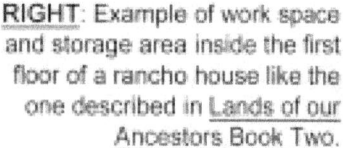

RIGHT: Example of work space and storage area inside the first floor of a rancho house like the one described in Lands of our Ancestors Book Two.

LEFT: Vaquero at work on a Mexican Rancho around 1830. - *Artist unknown. Image in public domain.*

RIGHT: Examples of Mexican Rancho cattle brands similar to the one described in <u>Lands of our Ancestors Book Two</u>.

LEFT: Example of a bull and bear fight similar to the one described in <u>Lands of our Ancestors Book Two</u>. These were common forms of entertainment for people of the Mexican Ranchos. -*"Sport in California, A Bull and Bear Fight" by Samuel Waller; Look and Learn/ Bridgeman Images*

Examples of Traditional California Native Structures

Chumash House - Ap (op)

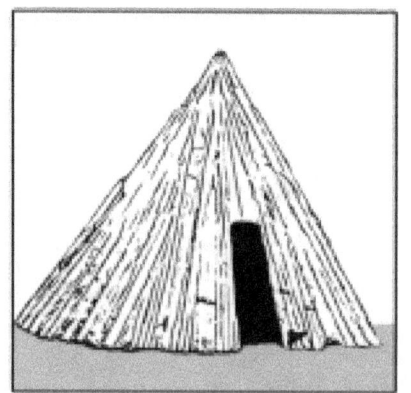

Styles of Yokuts Houses

One Example of Native Sweat House showing underground cutaway. Other similar designs were used by California tribes.

For Further Reading

Beebe, Rose Marie and Robert Senkewicz. Testimonios: Early California Through the Eyes of Women 1815-1848. Heyday Books, Berkeley, CA. 2006.

Bush Gibson, Karen. The Chumash, Seafarers of the Pacific Coast; Capstone Press, 2004.

Cook, Sherburne F. The Conflict Between the California Indian and White Civilization. University of California Press, 1976.

John P. Harrington's field notes from Maria Solares, Fernando Librado and other Native California consultants. Available through the J.P. Harrington Database Project located in the Culture Department of the Pechanga Tribe near Temecula, California.

Haas, Lisbeth Saints and Citizens: Indigenous Histories of Colonial Missions and Mexican California. University Press, Berkeley, California. 2014.

Miller, Joaquin. Unwritten History: Life Among the Modocs; Orion Press, 1972; first printed 1873.

Silliman, Stephen W. Lost Laborers in Colonial California: Native Americans and the Archaeology of Rancho Petaluma. University of Arizona Press, Tucson, 2004.

Timbrook, Jan. Chumash Ethnobotany: Plant Knowledge Among the Chumash People of Southern California. Santa Barbara Museum of Natural History, Santa Barbara, 2007.

Chumash Revolt of 1824 video. Chumash Science Through Time. Presented by Guadalupe Cultural Arts & Education Center. Directed and edited by Sabine Talaugon-Nicoles. 2018.

Book 2 Student Worksheets

Lands of Our Ancestors Book 2, Chapter 1

1. Describe Kilik's life after the missions. How old is he at the beginning of book 2? What is he doing? Where is he living?

2. Describe Tuhuy's life after the missions. How old is he at the beginning of book 2? What is he doing? Where is he living?

3. List some steps the Indians take to stay safe.

4. Describe the biggest responsibility you had when you were 14 and how it made you feel.

Lands of Our Ancestors Book 2, Chapter 2

1. What skills and knowledge do Kilik and Tuhuy develop in their new village?

2. How is the Place of the Condors different from a typical Native village?

3. Describe when you had to build new friendships with different types of people to get through a challenging time.

Lands of Our Ancestors Book 2, Chapter 3

1. Who is Kilik searching for? Why does it take so long to find them?

2. How do Kilik's search illustrate the difficulties for Native Americans today to trace their tribal identity?

3. Do you agree with the way Kilik decided to deal with the loss of his wife, unborn child, and sister? Explain your reasoning.

Lands of Our Ancestors Book 2, Chapter 4

1. What major historical event takes place in this chapter?

2. In this chapter, other events occur that affect or have the potential to affect Native people in California. What are they?

3. Why do Kilik and Tuhuy give their children Spanish names? Why were they hesitant to do so?

Lands of Our Ancestors Book 2, Chapter 5

1. Describe how each of the three historical events in this chapter affected the Native people of California.

        The 1833 Spanish flu epidemic impacted California Indians . . .

        Mexican Independence impacted California Indians . . .

        Selling missions lands to ranchos impacted California Indians . . .

2. How do these two groups justify their rights to California land?

        The Europeans would say the land is theirs because . . .

        The Indians would say the land is theirs because . . .

3. What are the similarities and differences between missions and ranchos?

	Mission	Ranchos
How they made money		
Role of Indians		
How they got the land		

Lands of Our Ancestors Book 2, Chapter 6

1. What were two advantages for Indians at the ranchos compared to the missions?

2. Why did Tuhuy volunteer to be the Indian foreman at Rancho Caballero?

 A. Earn more money for himself

 B. Protect his people

 C. Best way to get his tribe's land back

 D. All of the above

3. If you were among this kidnapped group, how would you feel as you arrive at this rancho and observe and listen to what's in store for you?

Lands of Our Ancestors Book 2, Chapter 7

1. What were the skills and qualifications for becoming a vaquero?

To become a vaquero a boy had to be . . . .

The skills and knowledge they had to learn included . . .

2. Malik and Alapay are glad to master new jobs and form new friendships at the rancho. Describe how fitting into the rancho culture caused conflict for each of them.

Becoming a vaquero caused conflict for Malik.

His family . . .

The other vaqueros . . .

Becoming friends with the ranchero's daughter caused conflicts for Alapay. Her family . . .

The ranchero family . . .

3. Describe a time when you fit into two very different groups.

1. How could Diego benefit from helping Kilik free his family from the rancho?

2. What racial stereotype does Señora Pacheco's believe about Indians like Alapay?

3. How does Alapay prove Señora Pacheco's view about Indian culture wrong?

4. What evidence proves Alapay is becoming as good a healer as her father?

1. Why did the Mexican Ranchos capture grizzly bears?

2. Describe two ways Malik would identify with the grizzly bear.

3. What do Malik's actions in this chapter tell you about his character? In what way(s) is he similar to his father, Kilik?

Lands of Our Ancestors Book 2, Chapter 10

1. How does Magdalena show her bravery and strength?

2. What was Tuhuy's quick decision?

3. What skills and character traits does Alapay have that could assist her family?

Lands of Our Ancestors Book 2, Chapter 11

1. Where might 200 warriors have come from to assist Diego and Kilik in the attack?

2. Why did Kilik risk being caught by sneaking onto the rancho prior to the attack?

3. How did Kilik's trust of the stranger in the dark pay off?

Lands of Our Ancestors Book 2, Chapter 12

1. How could the Native laborers and servants justify taking horses and all the food and tools they could when they left Rancho Caballero?

2. Summarize the events that take place once the Natives arrive at the Hidden Place.

3. Why do you suppose Diego and Kilik stayed at the Hidden Place and prepared for another battle instead of leading an escape?

Lands of Our Ancestors Book 2, Chapter 13

1. Who shows their bravery by risking their own safety twice?

2. Why did some Native people fight _with_ the Mexican troops?

3. Compare and contrast the risks and rewards of the Mexican troops with those of the Native warriors in this "final showdown."

Lands of Our Ancestors Book 2, Chapter 14

1. What does Solomol mean when he says "The floodgates have been thrown wide open?"

2. How does Solomol keep his family 'hidden' after leaving the Hidden Place?

3. Based on what you know about California history, predict what will happen to the Native people who stayed behind at the Hidden Place.

Book 2 Worksheet Answer Keys

Chapter 1 Answer Key
1. Kilik is 14 years old, but he is still very much a leader. He takes action and risks to keep children safe, and he is skilled at hunting.

2. Tuhuy is 13 years old, but he is still very much a thinker. He comforts the sick and reassures the worried children. He remembers the words of his elders.

3. They choose a hidden spot near a creek to camp, stay off the main trails, and know whether or not it is safe to build a fire.

4. Class discussion opportunity about responsibility. How do they figure out what to do without much adult help?

Chapter 2 Answer Key
1. Kilik learns to ride horses. Tuhuy learns how to grow food and medicine.

2. The Place of the Condors is home to multiple tribes. Their language, houses, and way of life are a blend of Chumash and Yokut. They grow some Spanish food, and horses are corralled there. While before they traded with each other, now they are more united and work as one.

3. Class discussion opportunity about collaboration and finding strength in differences.

Chapter 3 Answer Key
1. Kilik searches for his parents. It takes a long time because people move and die without a trace. Many are only known by their mission name. Language barriers also make it hard. It is also risky because if Kilik is caught he could be enslaved or killed by soldiers. He has to avoid leading them back to the Place of the Condor.

2. New mission names are often identical and give little detail about tribal roots. Many people have died or moved away without any way to find them. Records are in Spanish and controlled by Missionaries.

3. Answers will vary.

Chapter 4 Answer Key
1. Mexico gained independence from Spain in 1821 and, thus, control over Alta California.

2. Spanish colonizers are building towns and ranches throughout California. The traditional plants and herbs gathered by Native people, as are the animals they would traditionally hunt, are disappearing. There is a drought.

3. Kilik and Tuhuy give their children Spanish names in case of future interactions with Californios or Mexican authorities and also to protect them from those who might harm them. The men are

hesitant to give their children Spanish names because they want to maintain their Chumash traditions rather than carry on the practice of the Spanish invaders.

Chapter 5 Answer Key

1. The 1833 Spanish flu epidemic impacted California Indians . . . thousands more died because they lacked immunity and didn't have access to medicines or knowledge.

Mexican Independence impacted California Indians . . . was a false promise of freedom and a return of their land.

Selling mission lands to ranchos impacted California Indians . . . were removed from missions and to find new ways to survive in the pueblos, interior tribes, or the newly created ranchos.

2. The Europeans would say the land is theirs because . . . they use legal and financial documents to prove ownership.

The Indians would say the land is theirs because . . .the Creator gave it to them as stewards. They would prove it with their ancestors who have lived on this land since time immemorial.

3.

	Mission	Ranchos
How they made money	*SAME. Hide & tallow and agriculture.*	*SAME. Hide & tallow and agriculture.*
Treated Indians	DIFFERENT. Controlled all aspects of their life.	DIFFERENT. Only controlled them economically.
How they got the land	DIFFERENT. Granted by the king temporarily.	DIFFERENT. Sold by the government permanently.

Chapter 6 Answer Key

1. Allowed to keep families together. Allowed to practice their traditional culture.

2. "B" - It was risky for Tuhuy to put himself in such a prominent position because he would be

blamed if anything went wrong, but he could try to control how the Native laborers would be treated.

3. Student responses will vary.

Chapter 7 Answer Key

1. Vaquero needed to be physically fit and risk takers since this was a dangerous job. Skills and knowledge included:
- riding a horse
- creating and controlling a reata or lariat
- rounding up and herding cattle
- separating cattle
- roping and tying a calf or steer
- branding and slaughtering cattle

2. Being a part of two different cultures sometimes means not being entirely accepted in either. Malik knows his father and uncle despise the Rancheros, so becoming a vaquero feels like he is betraying his family and Indian culture. It makes it hard for him to talk to his family. Being an Indian means the other vaqueros tease or bully him. He works with them every day, but is treated as an outsider.

Alapay is conflicted because she has found an ally of sorts in Magdalena, the ranchero's daughter. As nice as Magdalena may be to her, Alapay knows she is merely a servant and that the other members of Magdalena's family do not share such a compassionate view of her or the other servants. They have to keep their friendship secret to avoid being judged, punished and separated.

3. Answers will vary. This phenomenon is known as 'Third Culture'. There is an expanded student project on third culture kids.

Chapter 8 Answer Key

1. As a leader of a village of runaways, one might infer that Diego has just as much hatred for the invaders as Kilik does. As populations shrank, tribes who might have not gotten along in the past now formed alliances for their greater safety. So if Diego helps Kilik his village would gain loyal members and Kilik would owe him loyalty.

2. Señora Pacheco believes Indians like Alapay are uncivilized, dirty, and the reason why her daughter was sick.

3. Alapay is able to identify the right plants to use as medicine and heal Magdalena completely.

4. Alapay healed Magdalena all by herself. This was the first time she did it without her father's help.

Chapter 9 Answer Key

1. During round ups rancheros entertained guests with bear and bull fights.

2. Malik would have identified with the grizzly as an important part of his Chumash culture honored in songs and legends. He could have also identified with the bear who also suffered from the cruelty of the vaqueros and ranchero.

3. Student answers will vary, but may include: Malik cares about animals; he believes, as the Chumash do, that bears should be honored and respected. So, like his father, he follows traditional Chumash ways. He knows the bear song and uses it as Kilik once did. He also appears to sometimes act without thinking, as Kilik did when he was younger.

Chapter 10 Answer Key

1. Magdalena stands up for Malik and Tuhuy in front of her parents and all of their guests.

2. Tuhuy tries to protect his nephew Malik by taking his punishment.

3. Student predictions will vary but should include that Alapay has been taught by her uncle how to hunt and fight, and she also knows how to heal with plants. She knows the Samala Chumash language as well as some Spanish. She is kind and caring, as she took care of Magdalena; yet she is also determined.

Chapter 11 Answer Key

1. Former mission Indians, or interior tribes. All had chosen to try to live away from pueblos, missions, and ranchos. Survival put them in direct conflict with Mexicans. Attacking the rancho could help them survive by killing or intimidating the rancheros. They could have also benefited by getting more people, livestock, horses, food or equipment.

2. Without his visit, the Natives would not have known what was happening and would not have create an inside advantage in the fight.

3. The stranger could have ruined the plan; but he helped to prepare the workers and gave Kilik valuable information, like where his son and cousin were being held.

Chapter 12 Answer Key

1. Rancho Indian workers were typically paid 'in kind' with things instead of pay. Or, they could argue it was compensation for the abusive treatment and loss of their land.
2. They fortify the Hidden Place, attend to the sick and wounded, fight off Mexican attack, then leave before more reinforcements come back.
3. They stay and fight instead of running away because they know there aren't many safe places left.

Chapter 13 Answer Key

1. Alapay

2. To be on the winning side means they could minimize risk of loss, injury or death. They could also possibly benefit by earning favor and blending into the dominant culture.

3. Mexicans attacked to maintain control and reclaim lost property and labor. They could have been rewarded with more labor and prestige of victory. Natives fought to defend their lives. If they won, they could have been rewarded with a safe place to live undisturbed.

Chapter 14 Answer Key

1. When real floodgates open, there's no stopping the rush of water that comes through. This is a metaphor for the arrival of Europeans in California.

2. Hide in plain sight by wearing Mexican clothing and using Spanish names. Stay hidden on side roads, Indian trails, and travel at night.

3. Predictions will vary. America takes over California so Native people will not get to keep their land. They will have to move to cities or reservations.

Class Discussion Questions

Identity

1. When do choices shape a person's identity?
2. How can we hold onto our sense of identity in the face of negative stereotypes?

Community

1. How does growing up in a different community than your parents shape your identity?
2. Is it possible to belong to different communities?

Systems of Control

1. When do systems of control backfire and make alliances of enemies and strangers?
2. How can the economy, how people work and take care of themselves, be a system of control for an entire society?

Conflict & Resistance

1. How can being vulnerable and sharing a bit of your culture with a stranger be a form of resistance?
2. Have you ever stood up to your friends or family to defend an outsider?

Resilience

1. How does getting through multiple challenges help people become survivors?
2. What are the negative consequences of continued loss, betrayal, and attacks?

Student Projects

Third Culture Kids

In this book Malik, Alapay, and even Magdalena grow up in a different world than their parents or grandparents. How does that shape their sense of identity? In this project students will learn more about what it means to be a third culture kid and create art that defines their own identity.

Step One:
Watch the video: Growing Up Everywhere: The "Third Culture Kid" Experience
URL: https://www.youtube.com/watch?v=4PZ8EPCgcQo

Define Key Terms:
Code Switching _____

_____

Displacement _____

_____

Minority Culture _____

_____

Answer Questions:
1. Take notes as you watch the video about who is a third culture kid.
   (star the ones that apply to you)

2. Describe three positive characteristics and skills common to all TCK.
   (star the ones that apply to you)

3. Describe three challenging experiences TCK typically face.
   (star the ones that apply to you)

Identity Art Project

Answering the question; 'where are you from?'

Illustrate how your identity represents more than one culture in either a short film, poem or a collage. Include inputs that shaped you such as: events, geography, culture, family. Include the positive characteristics and challenges you starred above.

Write A Historical Fiction Short Story (ES 1, ES 2, ES 3, ES 4)

The battle scenes between Indians and Mexican soldiers depicted in Chapters 12 and 13 of Lands of our Ancestors Book Two are derived from the last three chapters of Elias Castillo's nonfiction book A Cross of Thorns and Edward D. Castillo's Native American Perspectives on the Hispanic Colonization of Alta California.

Directions: Read first-hand accounts of the 1824 Chumash Revolt from one Chumash, Soldier and Priest. Write notes as you go. Create fictitious characters' including a Spanish priest, a Mexican soldier, and a Chumash rebel. Start your short story in 1823 with situations that explain what caused the revolt. How did the characters react during the revolt? What happened to the characters after the revolt?

Primary Sources

Chumash Voices:
Only two first-person Native accounts of the Chumash Revolt exist. First was Luisa Ygnacio (1830-1923), a Barbareno Chumash born at Mission Santa Barbara whose husband and mother-in-law lived through the revolt. Second was Maria Solares (1842-1923), an Inseneo (Samala) Chumash Indian who heard many elders' stories of their memories of the revolt. Their accounts were reported to J.P. Harrington an American ethnographer primarily interested in preserving Native American languages.

Blackburn, Thomas. "The Chumash Revolt of 1824: A Native Account." *The Journal of California Anthropology* Vol 2, no. 2 (1975): pp 223-227. (Maria Solares, Insenio Band, Chumash)

Hudson, Travis. "The Chumash Revolt of 1824: Another Native Account from the Notes of J.P. Harrington" *Journal of California and Great Basin Anthropology*, Summer 1980. Vol. 2, No. 1. pp. 123-126. (Lusia Ygnacio, Barbaranio Band, Chumash)

Soldier Voices:
Lieutenant Jose Maria Estrada, who led the assault on La Purisima gives a detailed account of the military attack. Rafael Gonzalez wrote about his experience on the expedition to bring back the Santa Barbara Mission runaways.

Cook, S.F. "Expeditions to the Interior of California: Central Valley, 1820-1840" *Anthropological Records* Vol 20, No. 5 (1962) 155-57. (Rafael Gonzalez)

Engelhardt, Zephyrin. "Mission La Concepcion Purisima de Maria Santisima" McNally & Loftin. (1986) pp. 261-267 (Lt. Jose Maria Estrada)

Priests Voices:

The Catholic Church's perspective is seen in priests' reports and letters to their colleagues and supervisors. Father Ripoll of Mission Santa Barbara writes the most detailed account of his experience at Mission Santa Barbara and what he heard about the other missions. His supervisor, Father Vicente Sarria's version, is very similar to Ripoll. There is no written account from Father Rodriguez who stayed at Mission La Purisima with the Chumash for a month as a hostage/negotiator.

Beebe, Rose Marie and Robert Senkewiez. "The End of the 1824 Chumash Revolt in Alta California: Father Vicente Sarria's Account" _The Americas_, Vol 53, No 2. (October 1996). pp. 273-283.

Geiger, Maynard. "Fray Antonio Ripoll's Description of the Chumash Revolt at Santa Barbara in 1824" _Southern California Quarterly_, Vol 52, No 4. (December 1970) pp 345-364

Legacy of Mission & Rancho (ES 1, ES 2, ES 3, ES 4)

How do the Spanish missions and Mexican ranchos make California's history different from the rest of America? Complete the side-by-side timeline that identifies major events.

	American West Coast History	American East Coast History
13,000 years ago		
1542		
1607		Colony formed in Jamestown, Virginia
1620		Pilgrims land on Plymouth Rock
1754-63		French-Indian Wars
1769-1823		
1775-93		American Revolution
1803		Louisiana Purchase
1810-1821		
1833		

Show how Spanish Missions, Mexican Ranchos and Native Californian history can still be seen in the West Coast today. Include pictures for all three along with and brief explanations of the following items:

- Architecture
- Names of places
- Roads
- Religion
- People
- Economy

Lands of our Ancestors Book Three

The American Colonial Period

Historical Summary

This work of historical fiction depicts what might have happened to California Native Americans as Alta California transitioned from Mexican control in the 1840s to US/American control in 1850 and beyond. Although the characters and the specific plot are fictional, the people and events in the book are based on historical documents and the historical writings of non-fiction authors and scholars.

More specifically, for example, some of the details of the lives of California Indians during the Gold Rush era came directly from the non-fiction personal narrative <u>Unwritten History: Life Among the Modocs</u>, written by Joaquin Miller and first published in 1873. Facts regarding the campaigns to slaughter California Natives from the end of the Mexican-American War to the early years of California statehood came from early California newspapers and <u>An American Genocide: The United States and the California Indian Catastrophe</u>, written by Benjamin Madley, published in 2016.

However the period is depicted, the truth is that the Gold Rush and the early years of California statehood contributed heavily to the further destruction and devastation of Native American peoples, communities and cultures in the region that became known as California.

In the 1840s, more immigrants from the United States and other countries began to arrive in Alta California, and Mexico was having trouble maintaining control of the territory. At the same time, Mexico was also having territorial troubles in another region, Texas, as the United States aggressively sought to expand its own lands. This led to war between the U.S and Mexico.

The Mexican–American War took place from 1846 to 1848, but most of the fighting happened outside California. This war followed in the wake of the 1845 annexation of Texas by the U.S., after the Texas Revolution a decade earlier.

About the same time, troubles between American settlers and Mexicans in Alta California had begun in earnest. In June of 1846 a band of Americans revolted, took over the city of Sonoma and jailed the Mexican governor, Mariano Guadalupe Vallejo. They raised the "Bear Flag" for the first time in the state. Then, acting on information that the English and Russians were planning to move in, American Commodore John Drake Sloat anchored in Monterey, the capital of Alta California, and raised the American flag. Sloat and his crew met no resistance from those living in Monterey. Approximately one-third of the northern half of Mexico, including California, became part of the United States after the U.S. defeated Mexico in 1848.

Just as the war was ending, James Marshall, an employee of immigrant landowner John Sutter, discovered a little nugget of gold at Sutter's lumber mill on the American River in

Coloma, California. News of the discovery spread like wildfire worldwide, bringing some 300,000 gold-seekers to the territory. The sudden influx of money and people allowed American settlers quickly move toward statehood.

The effects of the Gold Rush were substantial. Whole indigenous societies were attacked, decimated and pushed off their ancient lands by gold-seekers, called "forty-niners" in reference to the peak year of the Gold Rush immigration, 1849. San Francisco was the primary arrival point for those coming by sea, and the sleepy seaside village morphed into a major metropolis within a few short years. Those traveling by land often came over the Sierra Nevada Mountains by stagecoach, wagon train and later, locomotive.

The Gold Rush also caused environmental destruction through the introduction of hydraulic mining in the 1850s, which clogged and polluted rivers throughout the state, at great cost to the farmers and Native American villages downstream.

In the political arena, in 1849, delegates from around California gathered in Monterey, then the capital, to write a constitution for the new state. That constitution copied substantial portions of constitutions of other states as well as the U.S. Constitution, but also contained original provisions. The new constitution was ratified by popular vote later that same year, and Congress made California the thirty-first state in September 1850. As settlers continued to flood the state, Native Americans continued to suffer. Native inhabitants were often forcibly removed from their tribal lands by incoming miners, ranchers and farmers. Additionally, more than three hundred massacres of California Indians were carried out, while disease and starvation also took a heavy toll.

The new state government encouraged the process by passing laws that stripped Indians of rights while enabling non-Indians to buy and sell Indians as laborers. California's first Governor, Peter Burnet, openly called for a "war of extermination" of indigenous peoples while the state legislature provided the means of funding militias to carry out this policy. Between 1850 and 1860, the state paid out around one and a half million dollars for "expeditions against Indians."

Major Dates

June 14 – July 9, 1846	American migrants lead the Bear Flag Revolt to declare California a free state.
1846-1848	Mexican - American War
24 Jan 1848	Gold discovered at Sutter's Mill.
2 Feb 1848	Treaty of Hidalgo signed ending war.
22 Apr 1850	The Extermination Act for the Governance & Protection of Indians Acts passed.
9 Sept 1850	California Becomes the 31st State in America.
1853	The U.S. government establishes military reservations for Indians.
1854	Capital moves from Monterey to Sacramento.
1855	Church gives a small portion of land back to Samala Chumash.
1861-1865	U.S. Civil War.
1865	President Lincoln grants the Catholic Church ownership of some of the missions.

Images of the Period

Larkin House, Monterey. Built three blocks from the bay in 1835 by American merchant Thomas Larkin. It was the first two-story house in Monterey. Larkin operated a store from the back of the house. This is **where Alapay reconnected** with her Mexican friend, Magdalena.

This is a typical horse-drawn cargo wagon like the ones described on page 36. These vehicles were the delivery trucks of their day.

Sutter's famous lumber mill at Coloma, CA, on the American River where gold flakes were discovered in January, 1848. Geological forces working over millions of years produced high concentrations of the metal in this region of California, which **was the ancient homeland of the** Nisenan Indian people.

Pictured to the left is a method of gold-mining known as sluicing. Water from a riverbed is diverted into the sluice, allowing miners to pan for gold in the river's dry gravel bed. Groups of miners maintained camps near rivers and **streams, tearing down and** rebuilding the sluices as they cleared all the gold from a section of the river.

This image portrays the hydraulic method of gold mining as depicted on page 128 of Lands of our Ancestors Book Three. Many of the methods of mining gold destroyed the environment and made it impossible for plants, animals and fish to survive nearby.

San Francisco, 1850. After the discovery of gold in Alta California, San Francisco was transformed from a sleeping little seaside village into a major international city within two years. **It was the main arrival point** for gold seekers traveling by sea from all over the world.

Single shot, muzzle-loading pistol like the ones captured by Kilik and the people of Tukuyun's village described in chapter four.

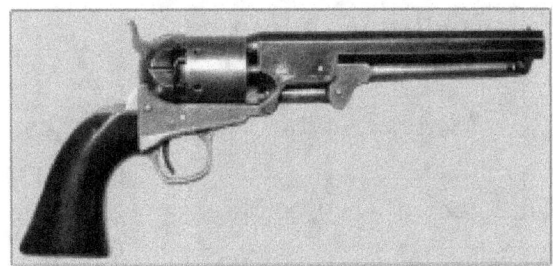

Colt 44 caliber revolver like the one Henry used to free Alapay on page 145. The single shot musket style pistol was no match for this innovation in weaponry.

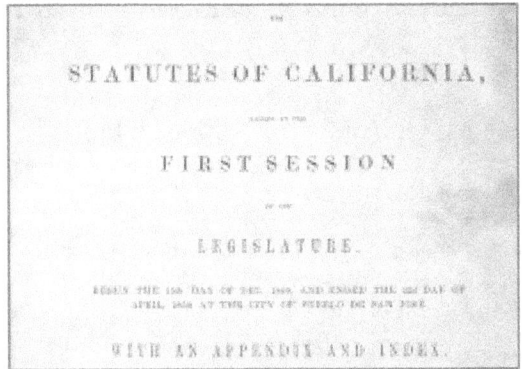

The newly created California state legislature wasted no time in passing laws that stripped Native Americans of their rights to land and liberty while giving other state citizens the ability to purchase Indians for labor.

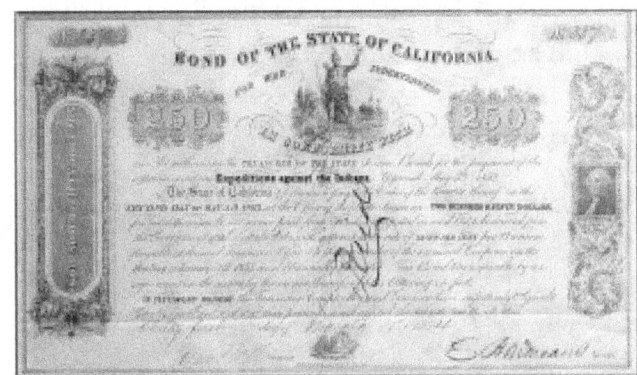

The new state government also provided the means to finance "Expeditions against the Indians" such as issuing bonds for sale to the public. This example bond had a value of $250. Around 1 million dollars was paid to militias that murdered thousands of California Indians.

These are the ruins of La Purisima Mission, which, like most of the Spanish missions, had been abandoned by the 1850s. As described on pages 171-174, Kilik's family passed by several mission ruins on their return journey to their homeland. A few California Indians **somehow managed to miraculously** survive the successive invasions of outsiders intent on taking the lands and resources of the area's original inhabitants.

For Further Reading

Rizzo-Martinez, Martin. We Are Not Animals; University of Nebraska Press. 2022.

Pitt, Leonard. The Decline of the Californios; University of California Press. Berkeley, CA 1966.

Madley, Benjamin. An American Genocide: The United States and the California Indian Catastrophe; Yale University Press, 2016.

Cook, Sherburne. The Conflict Between the California Indian and the White Population; University of California Press, 1976.

Heizer, Robert F.; The Destruction of California Indians; University of Nebraska Press, 1974; republished by Bison Books, 1993.

Book 3 Student Worksheets

Lands of Our Ancestors Book 3, Chapter 1

1. Why did Kilik, Tuhuy and their families leave the village known as the Hidden Place?

2. What is the reason Kilik and Tuhuy's families go in a different direction than Diego and his group?

3. Why is the necklace Kilik gives to Malik considered a powerful talisman?

4. Why did the group decide to put on dead people's clothes?

5. What gave away their secret to the soldiers?

Lands of Our Ancestors Book 3, Chapter 2

1. What natural features make the village, Place Above, such a safe place?

2. Why did the people from Place Above need to leave after years of relatively peaceful living?

3. As the group traveled northward how did they communicate safety and danger?

4. Why didn't the groups' disguises work on the Mexican soldiers they passed?

Lands of Our Ancestors Book 3, Chapter 3

1. What was the debate about the horses?

   a. Limik wanted to . . .

   b. Kilik and Malik wanted to . . .

2. What was the debate about the soldiers' caravan?

   a. Kilik wanted to attack because . . .

   b. Tukuyun didn't want to attack because . . .

3. How did they gain a strategic advantage?

Lands of Our Ancestors Book 3, Chapter 4

1. What does Kilik demand the Mexican man give him to complete his disguise?

2. What information did the prisoner have that was helpful to the Indians?

3. Why does Solomol suggest calling the stranger Tonto?

4. Why is Malik chosen to work with the prisoner?

Lands of Our Ancestors Book 3, Chapter 5

1. Why do Malik and Alapay want to go to Monterey?

2. What did the cousins do with Tonto when they arrived in Monterey?

3. The guns were useful to the people at the Place of the Sun because . . .

4. The guns were eventually useless because . . .

Lands of Our Ancestors Book 3, Chapter 6

1. Why would Alapay and Malik not know that Monterey is the capital of Alta California?

2. What was Alapay's surprise when she went looking for work at Mr. Larkin's?

3. Malik was not happy about his new job offer. Why did he think he should take it anyway?

4. What ceremony does Yol ask Tuhuy to perform? Why does Tuhuy have concerns about performing it?

Lands of Our Ancestors Book 3, Chapter 7

1. What does Magdalena teach Alapay that helps her spy on the Americans?

2. Why was Mariposa not supposed to talk to Mateo?

3. Why did Magdalena leave her father's big hacienda home?

4. Why does Mateo (Malik) start off lagging in the race?

Lands of Our Ancestors Book 3, Chapter 8

1. What caused conflicts between Native people and American strangers as they spread across the countryside?

2. During the raid at Rancho Buena Vista, why did Mateo have to fire his weapon?

3. Why were Mexican militias formed?

4. When does Mateo (Malik) stop cooperating with the rancheros?

Lands of Our Ancestors Book 3, Chapter 9

1. What problems did other Yokuts, who had already tried to move east, face?

2. What had changed in Miwok territory since Mariposa had been away?

3. Even though Tuhuy and Loknee came from different tribes, what did they have in common?

4. What did living among the Miwok people allow Tuhuy and Alapay to do?

5. What new California law said white settlers can kidnap, sell or enslave Native American people?

Lands of Our Ancestors Book 3, Chapter 10

1. Who was Henry Jamieson and why was he fascinated with indigenous people?

2. What prejudiced views had Henry heard about Indians?

3. Why won't the newspaper editor print stories about how badly Indians are being treated?

4. How was Alapay able to understand what the white men were saying?

Lands of Our Ancestors Book 3, Chapter 11

1. Why did Malik and Alapay travel to neighboring tribes' villages?

2. How does Malik know the attack on the village was by surprise?

3. How does Alapay know this attack was done by the white strangers?

4. What does Henry hope to learn from staying in Alapay and Malik's village?

Lands of Our Ancestors Book 3, Chapter 12

1. What did Malik call Henry that surprised Alapay?

2. What was so important about the faded images in the cave?

3. How did the cousins know the men with soldier uniforms on were not Mexican?

4. Why are the cousins worried no one will believe them?

Lands of Our Ancestors Book 3, Chapter 13

1. Why did Henry quit his job at the newspaper?

2. What does Alapay say to change her father's mind about trusting white men?

3. What does Henry tell the men to try and set Alapay free?

Lands of Our Ancestors Book 3, Chapter 14

1. What greeting gestures by Henry were unfamiliar to the people in the village?

2. How does Alapay prepare for the Eye of the Condor ceremony?

3. What did Alapay take with her for the ceremony?

4. How did Alapay recognize the Place of River Turtles during the ceremony?

Lands of the Ancestors Book 3, Chapter 15

1. Why do Solomol and Yol want to return to the Place of River Turtles?

2. Why does Henry's plan initially make everyone angry?

3. How will Henry's plan help the villagers as they travel?

Lands of Our Ancestors Book 3, Chapter 16

1. Why was Kai-ina able to guide them as they continued south?

2. What did Solomol do at the ruins of the mission where he and his family had lived some fifty years ago?

3. Why was the offering at the mission so important to the group?

4. Why didn't the native people they encountered speak their native languages anymore?

Book Three Answer Keys

Chapter 1 Answer Key

1. The Mexican military knew where the village was located. They would attack again.
2. They decided to go north where Kai-ina's people were from and had heard it was safer.
3. Talisman is a piece of deer antler blessed by a ceremonial leader from the Place of River Turtles that Malik had gotten from his father. It signified manhood, family and tribal connection.
4. Mexican clothes to disguise themselves as they traveled across open country.
5. Soldiers noticed they didn't have shoes on, which indicated they were Indians not true Mexicans.

Chapter 2 Answer Key

1. Long winding path that leads to a flat place that overlooks the valley below.
2. Signs in the night sky warned of danger. Sources of food and water were drying up.
3. Coyote wail means danger ahead. Magpie warble means all clear. Hawk screech warns 1 or 2 people coming.
4. It was suspicious they didn't have last names.

Chapter 3 Answer Key

1. Limik wants to eat the horses. Malik wants to ride the horses to scout.
2. Tukuyun didn't want to risk people getting killed. Malik wanted to free captives.
3. Captured firearms.

Chapter 4 Answer Key

1. Shoes
2. Mexican towns, movements and how to use firearms.
3. Because the padres had called native people this when they didn't understand.
4. Malik was chosen to speak to the prisoner because he spoke Spanish

Chapter 5 Answer Key

1. They heard there was rancho work there like they enjoyed before. Malik misses being a vaquero and Alapay liked working in the big rancho hacienda.
2. Dressed him as a Native, put him on a horse and sent the horse running through town.
3. Helped make hunting easier.
4. Ran out of gunpowder and could no longer be used.

Chapter 6 Answer Key

1. They have been living in a village far away and had never been there before.
2. Her old friend Magdalena worked there.
3. He would be valuable as a spy for his village.

4. A Condor Vision ceremony, which he has not performed in a long time and was worried it would not work.

Chapter 7 Answer Key

1. Teach her to read English so she can learn from the town signs and posters.
2. Natives were not allowed to talk to Mexicans. Malik, who used his Spanish name Mateo, was pretending to be a Mexican vaquero.
3. After the Indians escaped he became more bitter and unforgiving. She did not like being around him.
4. To avoid being pushed and shoved; trampled.

Chapter 8 Answer Key

1. Conflict over Native ancestral land claimed by colonizers land grants.
2. So the vaqueros would not think he was one of the natives.
3. Militias were formed to retaliate against raids. Raids often did not seek justice; slaughtered any Natives they found.
4. Malik leaves and warns the village before it is raided by the American militias.

Chapter 9 Answer Key

1. Disease and drought have taken a toll on food sources.
2. John Sutter built a fort and trading post which attracted more settlers.
3. Both of their names are Rain; Loknee means rain coming through, Tuhuy means rain.
4. They reconnected with nature and spiritual practices.
5. Act for the Government and Protection of Indians.

Chapter 10 Answer Key

1. Newspaper reporter who wanted to know how Indigenous people had lived for generations in California without ruining the land.
2. Indians are untrustworthy, dangerous, lazy and sneak up and rob you in your sleep.
3. Most readers wanted to hear about the booming economy because of gold.
4. She had learned English from Magdalena while she stayed at Mr. Larkin's.

Chapter 11 Answer Key

1. Malik and Alapay knew how to ride horses. To warn neighboring tribes about the trouble the new white strangers have brought.
2. The men died without weapons in their hands.
3. Alapay called on her spirit helper to reveal what had happened, and images began to appear to her of the events that took place.
4. Henry wants to record what the white men are doing to Natives and their land.

Chapter 12 Answer Key

1. Malik called Henry his friend.
2. The cave paintings reminded Alapay of Tuhuy teaching her Chumash symbols and their purpose.
3. They were white men, not brown. They wore blue, not red uniforms. They carried a

different flag.

4.   Doesn't seem possible, even to them.

Chapter 13 Answer Key

1.   His publisher refused to print Henry's story about the crimes against the Native Americans. He quit so he could write a book about it instead.

2.   Alapay says Mr. Larkin was another nice white man who was respectful to Indians.

3.   That she belongs to him because he paid for her.

Chapter 14 Answer Key

1.   Henry shook men's hands, and kissed ladies' hands.

2.   The night before, Alapay stayed quiet and focused her energy. The day of, she did multiple cycles of prayer and song.

3.   Tule reed mat and a basket water bottle.

4.   Her father had described where the Place or River Turtles was located.

Chapter 15 Answer Key

1.   Solomol and Yol are getting older and want to see their home village again.

2.   Henry's plan means they will have to pretend to be his slaves.

3.   Playing along with the American rules, helps them travel safely.

Chapter 16 Answer Key

5.   Why was Kai-ina able to guide them as they continued south?

• Recognized landmarks from her time living with the Yokuts.

6.   What did Solomol do at the ruins of the mission where his family lived?

• Offers a blessing song for the hundreds of Chumash who are buried there.

7.   Why was the offering at the mission so important to the group?

• Allowed them to acknowledge the pain and loss, which is the first step towards healing.

8.   Why didn't the native people they encountered speak their native languages?

• After living at the missions so long no one knew the language anymore.

Class Discussion Questions

Directions: Write one on the board for students to do a quick write at the beginning of class.

Identity

1. What are some ways that surviving three waves of colonization might have shaped how Indigenous people perceived themselves.

2. How can racial and ethnic stereotypes impact people's personal self image?

Community

1. Why would some parents hide their Indian heritage from their children during the early American period?

2. How did three waves of colonization change the nature of the Indigenous community?

Systems of Control

1. How did the narrative of the 'disappeared' Indian benefit American settlers?

2. How did the Expeditions Against Indians and the five dollar California State bond control the Indian population?

Conflict & Resistance

1. Why did the Catholic Church wait until the Americans took over to press the government to return the land to the Indians?

2. How did the California Gold Rush contribute to the outcome of the Civil War?

Resilience

1. Why does the truth help people heal?

2. What are some ways that people can honor their Native American heritage?

Student Projects

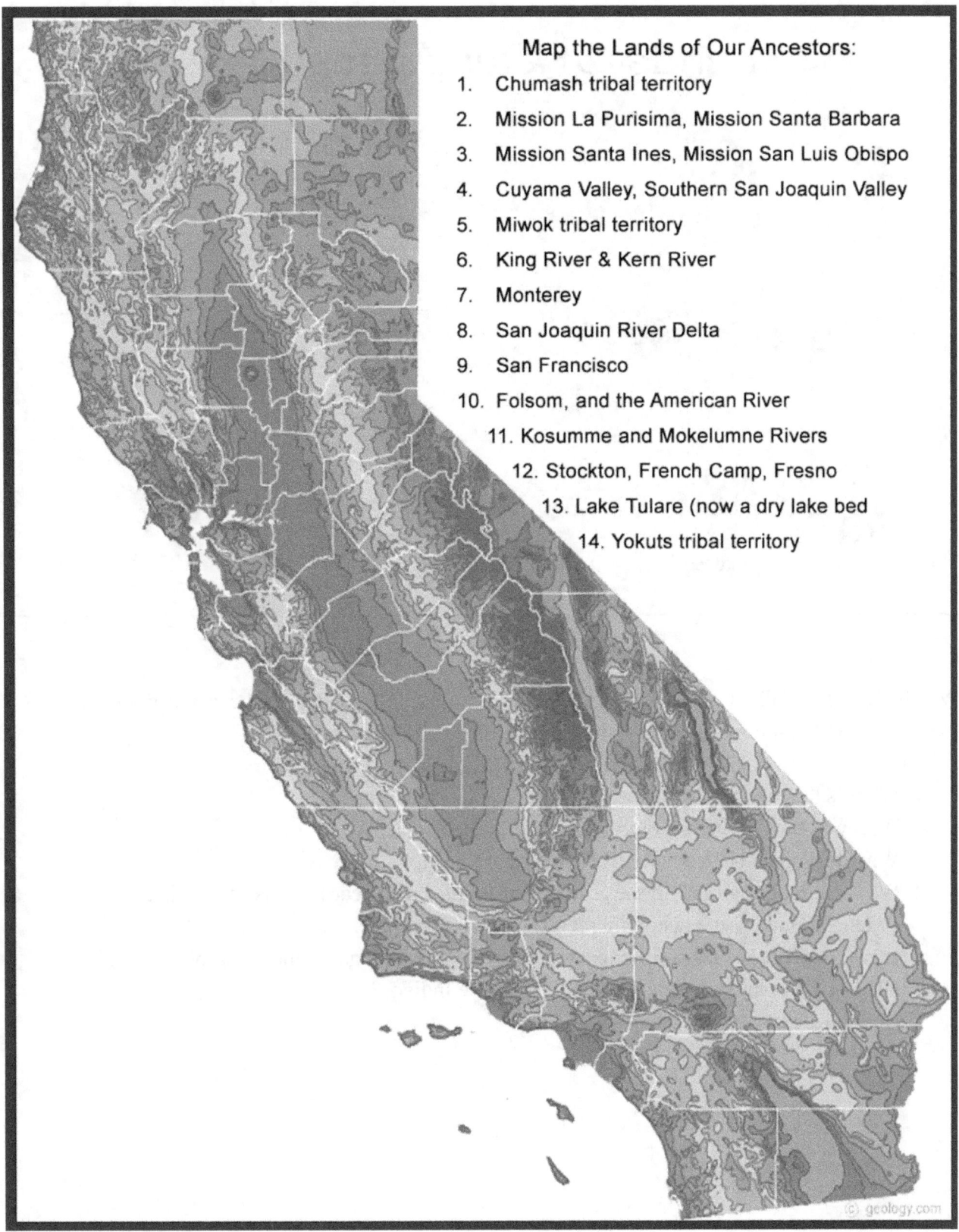

Map the Lands of Our Ancestors:

1. Chumash tribal territory
2. Mission La Purisima, Mission Santa Barbara
3. Mission Santa Ines, Mission San Luis Obispo
4. Cuyama Valley, Southern San Joaquin Valley
5. Miwok tribal territory
6. King River & Kern River
7. Monterey
8. San Joaquin River Delta
9. San Francisco
10. Folsom, and the American River
11. Kosumme and Mokelumne Rivers
12. Stockton, French Camp, Fresno
13. Lake Tulare (now a dry lake bed
14. Yokuts tribal territory

Native Roots

Lands Of Our Ancestors

Family Tree

Watch the video "Who Can Identify as a Native American?" and answer these questions.
(URL: https://www.youtube.com/watch?v=ZBQPks1zb3A)

1. What is the difference between biological and social kinship?
2. Why was the Dawes Act blood quantum created?
3. What test could be used to prove biological kinship?
4. What are registry rolls? In the case of California tribes near the missions, what organization kept the historical records for tribal membership?
5. How does tribal citizenship impact people financially, legally and socially?
6. Historically, why did Americans pretend to be Indians?
7. How does this harm real Indians?

We Are Still Here

Resilience: *the capacity to withstand or to recover quickly from difficulties; toughness.*

Watch this Ted Talk "Changing the Way We See Native Americans" about Matika Wilbur's 2013 Project 562 to photograph members of each Federally recognized tribe in the United States. (URL: https://www.youtube.com/watch?v=GIzYzz3rEZU)

"My dream," Wilbur says, "is that our children are given images that are more useful, truthful, and beautiful." Identify four examples of resilience from her talk. Write a brief summary of each below.

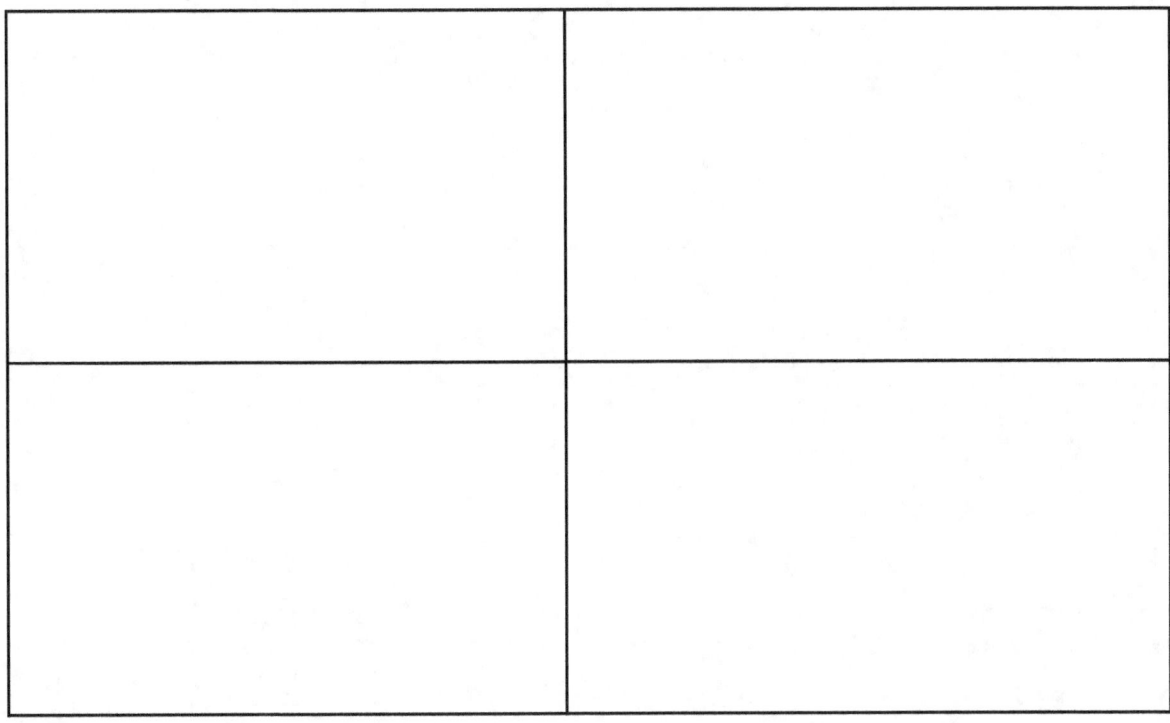

Next, do some research about the California tribe in your community. What are three ways they are demonstrating resilience?

www.ingramcontent.com/pod-product-compliance
Lightning Source LLC
Chambersburg PA
CBHW080752120626
46557CB00005B/1240